April, 13, 2011

To Melissa,

thank you for going beyond the call of duty – for your kindness and compassion.

May you always hear your own drumbeat.

Marian D. Kelley

DRUMBEATS
FROM

DRUMBEATS FROM MESCALERO

A list of all books currently available in this series may be found in the back of this book.

Mescalero

CONVERSATIONS WITH APACHE ELDERS, WARRIORS, AND HORSEHOLDERS

H. HENRIETTA STOCKEL
with MARIAN D. KELLEY

TEXAS A&M UNIVERSITY PRESS
COLLEGE STATION

First edition
This paper meets the requirements of
ANSI/NISO Z39.48–1992
(Permanence of Paper).
Binding materials have been chosen for durability.

Library of Congress Cataloging-in-Publication Data

Stockel, H. Henrietta, 1938–
Drumbeats from Mescalero : conversations with Apache elders, warriors, and horseholders / H. Henrietta Stockel with Marian D. Kelley.—1st ed.
p. cm.—(Elma Dill Russell Spencer series in the West and Southwest ; no. 37)
Includes bibliographical references and index.
ISBN 978-1-60344-230-5 (hc-stamped with jacket : alk. paper) 1. Apache Indians—New Mexico—Mescalero Indian Reservation—Interviews. 2. Apache Indians—New Mexico—Mescalero Indian Reservation—History. 3. Mescalero Apache Tribe of the Mescalero Reservation, New Mexico. I. Kelley, Marian D. II. Title. III. Series: Elma Dill Russell Spencer series in the West and Southwest ; no. 37.
E99.A6S74 2011
979.004′9725—dc22

2010043647

For Lorrie and Selah, so they will know . . .

For Lynne, my son John, and future sons and daughters of the Apache nation who live on the Mescalero Reservation. May they always hear the drumbeats.

Hope is the pillar that holds up the world.

—Pliny the Elder (23–79 AD)

TABLE OF CONTENTS

PREFACE

Most Americans know that during a significant period of settling the West, the name "Apache" carried such meaning that it became an integral part of our nation's history that has endured until today. Behind the legend were hundreds of men, women, and children—the sons and daughters of true American heroes like Mangas Coloradas, Cochise, Victorio, Geronimo—whose actions in defending their way of life had their roots in tribal history. By the time this latest group came along, it was an old story. For centuries, before the first American footprint hit the soil of Apacheria, thousands of Spanish and Mexican peoples had occupied the same territory and had been the target of Apache resistance. Now the pioneers and entrepreneurs from the eastern states were simply the latest group to covet the climate and resources of the Apache homelands; like its Hispanic predecessors, the American juggernaut was on the move.

Since then the generic word "Apache" has become immortal, infamous, and glamorized or romanticized by more than one hundred years of constant media interest—newspapers, pulp fiction, film, magazine articles, history books, radio, television, and even the military. The name "Geronimo" has been yelled as paratroopers jump from airplanes, and the Apache helicopter has become an important fighting tool in twenty-first century American warfare. On America's side, paradoxically.[1]

In the minds of many Americans, however, Apache history stopped short when Geronimo surrendered in 1886 and the entire band of more than five hundred Chiricahua Apaches was imprisoned for twenty-seven years. For a time reports of the incarcerated Apaches' activities were newsworthy, particularly for members of Indian rights organizations whose passion for justice motivated their interest, but the general public eventually went on its way, aware of the Chiricahuas but not as involved as it had been.

Very little attention through the years had been devoted to the other bands of Apache peoples, those not as sensationalized. For example, at the time of the Chiricahua Apaches' imprisonment, hundreds of San Carlos and White Mountain Apaches were on their own reservations in Arizona, as were the Jicarilla Apaches in northern New Mexico. Important to this book, however, a group known as the Mescalero was peacefully going about life on the Mescalero Apache Reservation. It is here, in the high desert pine forests of south central New Mexico, that most of the surviving two hundred plus Chiricahua prisoners, upon release in 1913, would call home. It is here also that socialization and intermarriages would bring together the once separate Mescalero, Lipan, and Chiricahua peoples. The twelve Apaches whose interviews are the purpose of this book are descendants of any one, two, or three of these bands. Some interviewees bring outside genetic heritages and influences as well. In this regard they are not unlike many other Americans from the dominant society, but only in this way. Readers will become familiar with the stark contrast the lives of contemporary Apaches present. Broadly speaking, nothing has changed; they are still pariahs, still stigmatized by a government seeking revenge for their ancestors' resistance to American imperialism.

AUTHOR'S NOTE

This is an informal book of interviews, written and compiled by friends about friends. Yes, it does follow a few academic standards, but by and large there were no boundaries, no structured format that we routinely observed. It is a different type of book about Apaches, one that varies considerably from most previously written nonfiction tomes, and especially from pulp fiction portrayals and Hollywood's brutal characterizations. Within these pages you will hear contemporary Apaches discussing their concerns about life on the reservation, about the future of the tribe, and about the hope they carry in their hearts for their people and for the tribe's survival amid the nearly overwhelming challenges of the early twenty-first century. It is a new way for me to present the history and culture of the Mescalero, Chiricahua, and Lipan people, and through it I have gained even more respect and admiration for these descendants of one of the most famous Indian tribes in American history.

At certain times during the day a local public radio station in Las Cruces, New Mexico, broadcasts information about the next day's road closings at specific sites on Highway 70 as it crosses the sweeping Plains of San Agustin. A driver comes upon the magnificent valley, stretching from left to right as far as the eye can see, immediately after noting a sign announcing the altitude of the mountain pass—a little more than 5,700 feet. Brushed in muted shades of lavender, gray, brown, and green, the Plains below were named by early Spaniards, surely awed by the sight, for Saint Augustine. The road closings are devoid of any religious connection but are due to deadly missiles being periodically test-fired by the United States Army over the valley, now renamed the White Sands Missile Range.[1] The contrast is both profound and profane.

Four thousand Apaches live on the Mescalero Apache Reservation, about one hundred miles beyond the mountains that protect the far northeastern region of the Plains. On July 16, 1945, the hot wind from a nuclear explosion at Trinity Site on the missile range raged furiously across that reservation, killing hundreds of livestock and causing sickness among the descendants of some of the most famous Apache heroes in American history. Religious images produced in the rational mind by the word "Trinity" have absolutely no relation to a bomb; the motive for U.S. government's naming the killing field after Christianity's most sacred icons has never been revealed. Nonetheless, speculation abounds.[2]

The striking insensitivity regarding the selection of a name does not surprise the Apaches, weary veterans of political actions, society's insults, and stereotypical judgments. The many aspects of their often-contentious relationships with the federal government and their evolving connections with the surrounding white society are some of the topics addressed in this book. These oral narratives became history the moment they were spoken. In that regard, they also create a cultural context within a temporal benchmark, establishing for future generations the particular circumstances affecting this small but varied group of tribal members in 2008. My dear friend and traveling companion, Marian Kelley, and I are honored and privileged to be the chroniclers, the facilitators, enabling these speakers to forge and occupy their individual niches in Apache history through their words.

As so often happens in writing a book, the original intentions go astray. To start, my plan was to interview only Chiricahua Apaches because they are the group on the Mescalero Apache Reservation with whom I am most familiar. In time, the scope of this work necessarily broadened to include members of the two other Apache groups also—the Mescalero and the Lipan. These different bands of once-free-roaming American Indians have lived together for nearly a century on the Mescalero Apache Reservation and by now have much in common, so the distinction is no longer as perceptible as it once was, at least in terms of how they view themselves and their current situations.

Somewhere along the way Marian added her thoughts to the interviews as they were being conducted. Her questions and comments were so insightful and so relevant that she became indispensable to me and to the project. Thus, Marian has joined me in producing this book even though our outlooks occasionally were at odds. For example, I was more pessimistic than she, believing many of the Apache respondents were in emotional pain because of their ancestors' trauma and their own uncertain future. I made a mental leap from there to the conclusion that the tribe was in danger of annihilation, no longer by violence from the guns and soldiers of the historical American West, but by ruthless modern social weapons wielded by the U.S. government and its agent, the dominant white society. Marian pointed out that she and most of the Apaches we interviewed were optimistic, hopeful, and able to cope with the impact of the government's actions and modern-day life amid the surrounding culture; nonetheless, she had concerns. She was right, and I was surprised to detect a common thread running through these interviews with twelve Apaches of different ages and perspectives: hope for the tribe's future.

Our interview style was "conversational" and our approach was tailored to the individuals being interviewed. So, not all the questions to each speaker were similar, but all the responses were candid and are reported just as they were given. Of necessity, some of our questions to elders, for example, differed from our inquiries to the much younger horseholders. Nonetheless, spontaneity, from them and us, was crucial and often led our speakers and us into unanticipated areas of concern or hopefulness. Structured inquiries and pseudo-sophistication in all of its forms were deliberately left at the door; these were talks among trusted friends. The same informal approach was used for the photos. They were candid shots, not posed. Some interviewees were self-conscious about being photographed, but cooperated nevertheless, even if it required cajoling.

We told the speakers in advance of the two related topics we wanted them to address if they were agreeable: the possibility of continuing governmental ethnocide/genocide against the Apaches, and the future of the tribe. Everyone said "yes." One early contact, however, refused our request for an interview, citing a possible adverse affect on his business should he express his honest views. We understood. Another friend was not a good choice because he lived off the reservation and thus wasn't deeply involved with the daily routine there; he excused himself.

In subsequent interviews our friends discussed many subjects, related or unrelated directly to our questions. If some of their answers seem to stray from the basic topics, they do, often sliding into unexpected areas. We attributed these comments to ancestral speaking patterns, for example, Apaches don't address basic themes immediately. Rather, they wait until they are ready, bringing out many different opinions about varying topics first. Readers will also note that some of the speakers did not specifically respond to our inquiries, as is customary in the dominant society. Out of a deep and abiding respect, we didn't force the matter. Those unfamiliar with Native American conversations may think the two basic premises were ignored in certain interviews, but the Apaches referred to the issues, no doubt about that, even though some answers remain hidden behind other subjects.

Each speaker was asked to suggest solutions to the problems he or she identified. Some responded to that request, some didn't, but none of the Apaches used this forum as a "gripe session." Instead, many of their words clearly describe the obvious, current examples of what they and I consider to be a long history of cultural destruction, or even a modern-day equivalent of the genocide that occurred centuries ago. In many ways the federal government's actions and white society's influences still today continue to define the tribe as subordinate; the meaning and implementation of sovereignty has been lost, if it ever was a factor in the lopsided power association.

Before each interview, our speakers were told that they were in complete control of the material. Afterward, each respondent was given a copy of the "raw" interview just as I transcribed it from the audiotapes. After they reviewed and changed it, in some instances, I retyped the information, incorporating their edits, and returned it for one final inspection. Consequently, the individual whose words and photos are on the pages in front of you approved the information contained in this book.

Readers may consider some opinions to be controversial or even outrageous, but I definitely believe that trained non-Indian historians, authors, researchers, Apache aficionados, and other outsiders do not have the moral authority to evaluate the Apaches' opinions, either quantitatively or qualitatively. Marian and I agree completely with American Indian authors Clara Sue Kidwell, Homer Noley, and George "Tink" Tinker who recognize that "Western categories do not work for identifying and describing, naming, or explaining Indian . . . realities."[3] I have come to deeply appreciate, understand, and agree with the meaning of that quote. However, that is not to say that I don't respect the scholars and their works that have, in the past, defined the Native American experience for readers. Many of those books opened the door to a mountain of information that needed to be explored from the alternate point of view—the perspective held by American Indians, in this case the Apache people. Nonetheless, not enough credence was given to the Indian side of the story, possibly because oral history had not achieved a reputable position in historiography. Still, there were those whose interest was high enough to meet the challenge.

In 1930, anthropologist Harry Hoijer appeared on the Mescalero Apache Reservation, tablet and pencil in hand ready to ask compliant

Apaches to tell him their myths and stories. He didn't know them and they didn't know him, but ultimately he performed somewhat of a miracle in convincing a few individuals to cooperate. His book, *Chiricahua and Mescalero Apache Texts,* was published in 1938.[4]

Around the same time, Morris Opler, a University of Chicago anthropologist, found favor with a number of Apaches and collected diverse oral materials. His book, *An Apache Lifeway,*[5] originally published in 1941, is considered the trailblazer as it is more expansive than Hoijer and has become *the* comprehensive study of the Chiricahua culture from the point of view of Apaches in the early to middle twentieth century.

In the late 1940s, Eve Ball, a resident of Ruidoso, New Mexico—the town that abuts the northern boundary of the Mescalero Apache Reservation—befriended the Apaches and through her kindness, neighborliness, and unmistakable sincerity began to interview the next generation, some of whom had been, by then, educated in boarding schools. The Apaches learned to trust "Mrs. White Eyes" and gradually revealed the truth, as they lived and learned it, of the historical events that affected them, their parents, and grandparents. Ball's book, *Indeh: An Apache Odyssey,*[6] was published in 1980 and has become a modern classic.

Between then and now, a few authors, myself included, have talked with and received permission to quote numerous Apaches in our books. Still, this is the first time in sixty years that certain Apaches have agreed that their concerns will be represented through the written word. They are aware of their history being misinterpreted and their tribal information mismanaged, and know that they, their ancestors, and their culture have been evaluated, judged, and disparaged by some who utilize a significantly different set of values. This and many other hurts have had quite an adverse impact.

Like Hoijer, Opler, and Ball, this book is only what it purports to be—a series of interviews by our friends who are, not incidentally, also members of the Mescalero Apache Tribe. Some of these Apaches are Mescaleros by heritage, some Chiricahuas, and some Lipans. By now many have the bloodlines of all three bands.

I cannot stress strongly enough the importance of understanding that this book is not a comparative study that uses acceptable academic standards or guidelines. I do not contrast the contemporary Apache culture with any other Native American society or with the so-called American way. Instead, the interviews stand alone, and that is all I intend them to do. To design and attempt to implement anything else would have been unrealistic and impractical because the Apaches would probably not have cooperated. As a matter of fact, it has taken the last twenty-five years of friendships to gain the trust that led to acquiring the concurrences necessary to begin this project.

Our conversations started in early December of 2007, and the last interview was held at the end of January 2009. The discussions are a "snapshot in time," and each is dated for the reader. Taking into consideration today's fast-paced society, unanticipated events may have subsequently happened to the speakers in between the time we talked and the time of publication. Nonetheless, no one has asked to bring the interview up to date.

Prior to approaching our friends, I theoretically grouped the interviewees into three separate categories: elders, the middle-aged, and young adults or, as Marian has offered—the elders, the warriors, and the horseholders. I limited the respondents to twelve people, out of regard for the twelve poles that support a sacred tipi in which part of the annual puberty ceremonies are conducted. Thus, this book can be considered to have a spiritual basis. When I initially approached the interviewees and revealed why I had chosen twelve persons for interviews, they all agreed that their participation would be enhanced and symbolized by the meaning of the number twelve. This proposed affiliation with a sacred aspect of their culture was instrumental in obtaining concurrence for the testimonies. Metaphorically speaking, it can be inferred that these individual speakers are in many ways supporting their culture amid the whirlwinds and challenges of the first decade of the twenty-first century.

Some of the Apaches you will meet are college-educated men and women, some high school graduates or dropouts, some hold professional positions, one is a medicine man, one a religious Sister, one a tribal judge, one a student. Some are from the same prominent families, a deliberate choice. In the historical Apache way, certain families have always held leadership positions, whether those holdings are tacit, explicit, do or don't reflect the dominant culture's hierarchal structure. It is still that way. And so you will meet a brother and sister—Ed and Sister Juanita Little, descendants of a stolen child who was raised by the Mescalero Apaches. You will meet a grandmother, Kathleen Kanseah, and her grandson Dan and granddaughter Eliza, descendants of warriors. You will meet another grandmother, Claudine Saenz, and her granddaughter Kiana Mangas, descendants of Mangas Coloradas and Victorio. Regardless of their heritage, all the interviewees share a collective history of their ancestors—Mescalero, Chiricahua, and Lipan—being formidable enemies of the United States in the not-too-distant past.

My use of terms is important to understand. References to Mescalero, Chiricahua, and Lipan Apaches are synonymous. The words "white man," or "white society," or any similar uses of the word "white" represent the U.S. government and the dominant society. The context will supply the meaning.

Before continuing, it will be helpful to explain the meaning behind the subtitle "Conversations with Elders, Warriors, and Horseholders." Among most Apaches, elders are viewed with great respect, are treated with high regard, and are taken care of in many ways by their families and the tribe. Our selection of these four specific elders—Kathleen Kanseah, Edward Little, Sister Juanita Little, and Claudine Saenz, was deliberate. We have observed over many years' time the honored manner in which these particular elders are held by other Apaches. Intimidating as it can be to approach them and ask for interviews, we are fortunate to have their cooperation.

As for the warriors, each of them in their own way—Joey Padilla, Depree Shadowwalker, Alfred LaPaz, Debi Martinez, and Larry Shay—has courageously spoken out, documenting circumstances within the tribe as they interpret them. They are the spiritual descendants of fighters whose fearlessness in battle protected the tribe from the government's military actions against them. Unlike their ancestors, however, these warriors use different weapons, believing that words, and the subsequent attention they could attract and relief they might subsequently bring, may help alleviate the daunting situations affecting the contemporary tribe. In their hearts these warriors hold the same hope for relief their ancestors did when confronted with nearly overwhelming obstacles to their survival as a people. These speakers are the incarnation of those famous historical Apache men and women who were willing, at any cost, to defend the tribe's basic right to survival. Their modern fight starts here.

And, lastly, an explanation of the term "horseholders." During the time of freedom, Apache warriors and tribesmen had apprentices known as "horseholders." In essence, these young men [unfortunately, no women] were valets of a sort, tending to their mentors' horses, cooking, clothing, moccasins, and weapons. In turn, the warriors taught their novices all that was necessary to become fighters, including warfare tactics and strategy, the special language of the battle, the ways to care for the implements and animals of war, methods of protecting the tribe from harm, techniques used to keep the women and children safe, and how to behave when in the company of heroes. After the lessons were learned and the prescribed physical trials were held, most of these boys would graduate to become warriors themselves and would ultimately take on apprentices, thus continuing the tradition and heritage. Today's horseholders—Dan Kanesah Jr., Eliza Yuzos, and Kiana Mangas—are not assigned to any particular warrior, but their obligations as future leaders of the tribe remain unchanged, perched somewhere beyond the horizon, waiting patiently for them to mature and move into place.

So now, with a bow of respect for the elders, applause for the modern-day warriors, and pats on the backs of the horseholders, it is time to begin.

DRUMBEATS FROM MESCALERO

INTRODUCTION

Still in Survival Mode

The Apaches you are about to meet are storytellers of a sort, not exactly in the traditional understanding of that designation and its obligations,[1] but they are in the forefront of Indian peoples all across America who are speaking out for themselves. Too often, in years past, outsiders wrote their history; now some indigenous peoples are documenting their history and current situations, which is as it should be. It must be remembered that not too long ago their ancestors were dehumanized, characterized as savages, barbarians, less than fully human. They were prohibited from expressing their concerns, from criticizing those in authority; the punishment was often death.

Not all contemporary Apaches are interested in talking about their history and their lives. Although some are still reluctant, those who consented to be interviewed by us are not among the reticent. As silly as it sounds in the twenty-first century, it is important to demythologize the stereotypes that have endured over the centuries. The Apaches whom you will come to know in this book are mothers, fathers, sisters, brothers, uncles, aunts, grandmothers, and grandfathers and contain within themselves all manner of the complex attributes that comprise a human being. They laugh and cry, celebrate birthdays and anniversaries, have hopes and dreams, fears. The Apache people catch colds, cook dinner, forget to fill the gas tank, owe utility bills, go to church, and win and lose arguments. Some of them can forgive what was done to their ancestors; some cannot. Some contradict themselves in these interviews; some do not. And so on.

Additionally, each of the speakers has had a hand in addressing, alleviating, complicating, or doing nothing about the circumstances they meet during the course of each day. In that way, they are responsible for helping to bring about a future for the tribe. Or not.

Most of these Apaches acknowledge that there are a number of obstacles that must be surmounted in order to reach a time free of today's impediments; they will tell you about those. Many who talked with us inferred that they are a people and a culture adrift, still affected by a toxic white society and adversarial relationships with successive political administrations, even after more than one hundred years. In the words of Sister Juanita Little, OSF, a Mescalero religious woman, "We are still in survival mode."[2]

Without a doubt her comment clearly identifies the enduring consequences of colonization by Spanish, Mexican, and American governments; military personnel; and religious institutions, all of which exercised conspicuous imperialism and a moral and ethical disregard for the history and culture of the Apache people. These reprehensible actions are documented, objective, and established. Of significant interest and also well defined is the Apaches' adaptation to the Euro-American enemies.

For example, shifting alliances was the overt pragmatic cultural trait exercised by some of the speakers' ancestors on the Spanish colonial frontier. To thwart the conquistadors' policies of enslaving or killing Apaches who wouldn't acquiesce to their demands, certain captives learned and imitated the ways of the Europeans' culture, even openly practiced Roman Catholicism, and became role models of behavior.[3] In their hearts, however, fidelity to their ancient ways remained paramount and emerged once the danger had passed.

Adjustment to threatening situations was again apparent on the Mexican frontier when Apaches entered into agreements with this latest generation of encroachers. By helping Mexico's pioneers improve their horse and cattle herds—stealing from Peter to pay Paul, so to speak—freely roaming Apaches became the entrepreneurs of northern Mexico's cattle industry and survived by creating a multiethnic trading alliance that extended northward into New Mexico's pueblo country and as far eastward as the Comanche lands in Texas.

American occupation of historic Apache lands was the next menace that brought forth a hearty dose of pragmatism. When the great swarm of city-dwelling easterners migrated westward in the middle to late 1800s, new confrontations were the result of bald-faced U.S. expansionism, stoked by a catchy slogan of "Manifest Destiny."[4] Many Apaches resisted the incursion while others realistically and peacefully capitulated,[5] reconciling themselves to outlasting yet another genocidal upheaval.

In 1873, the Mescalero Apaches, still not fully recovered from their deadly experience at Bosque Redondo,[6] reluctantly accepted a small portion of their vast territory near New Mexico's Sacramento Mountains as a "reservation."[7] The Lipan group, militarily displaced from their homelands in West Texas, joined their relatives and friends on the reservation in the early 1900s. When the last Chiricahua holdouts—Geronimo's band—surrendered in 1886, the entire mighty Chiricahua Apache nation of more than five hundred men, women, and children was unlawfully restrained and incarcerated for twenty-seven years. No one in authority bothered to note that the imprisonment was in direct violation of the legal guarantee provided all peoples of America, regardless of ethnic background, by the writ of habeas corpus.

Upon release from confinement in 1913–14, a small number of Chiricahua Apaches remained in Oklahoma and the rest were transferred to Mescalero. In the eyes of the government, the illegal imprisonment back in 1886 signaled that the Apache wars had ended and, after nearly three decades of confinement during which the infamous Geronimo had died, the government felt secure enough to release the prisoners. But the Apache wars had not ended, had not been relegated to the dusty pages of history books. Appearances to the contrary, the battles continue today, using contemporary methods but with the same direct and indirect goals—the extermination of the Apache people.

Whether the speakers' noble heritage coupled with their ancestral legacy of endurance and mental and physical superiority will enable today's Mescalero, Chiricahua, and Lipan Apaches to overcome the twenty-first century's trials remains unknown and speculative. However, as Marian Kelley and I believe, with their ancestors' spirits remaining rooted in their bones and blood, there is no doubt they will succeed. And definitely, if hope continues to live in their strong hearts, they will succeed. They will tell you that. That's what this book is all about.

THE SPEAKERS

The governments of Spain, Mexico, and the United States did everything in their power to completely exterminate the ancestors of our speakers, and failed. As time is passing, only the transmitted stories of those events remain in many families; actual contact with relatives who had the experiences and bore the pain of those times has, for the most part, vanished into history. Fortunately, there are still exceptions. For example, Chiricahua Apache elder Kathleen Kanseah still clearly recalls her father-in-law, Jasper, Geronimo's youngest warrior and nephew. He sits on the top row left in the well-known 1886 photo of the train that was carrying the recently surrendered Geronimo's band to prison in Florida. Freed from confinement as an adult, Jasper Kanseah lived out his days at Mescalero embraced by the love of his immediate and extended family, Kathleen included. But, as is typical, she doesn't talk much about him.

Even though Apaches have always been reticent to share their tragic history with outsiders, and will think long and hard before discussing protected information, the late Eve Ball was a special friend to the Apaches and an exception. All western historians and Apache aficionados should appreciate her book, *Indeh: An Apache Odyssey,*[1] a series of interviews mainly with the sons and daughters of the great ones who tell her their "side." Prior to that, however, there is no similar first-person historical record of the circumstances written by Apaches describing their contact with Europeans on the Spanish and Mexican colonial frontiers,[2] and that is a significant lapse in the overall history of this tribe.

In the next pages you will read the testimonies of elders, the middle-aged warriors, and the horseholders under thirty years of age. Very little editing has been done and so the words clearly reflect the personalities of each speaker. All are different from one another, all are willing to share their statements with you, and all are proud of their heritage.

We begin with four highly respected individuals, elders by age but more than that by respect and the honored status they hold among the Apache people. One is a Chiricahua, two are Mescaleros, and one is Warm Springs.[3]

The Elders

Kathleen Kanseah

Marian Kelley interviewed Kathleen on a bright and cold day in January of 2008. They sat together at the Kanseah dining room table, truly one of those pieces of furniture that "if it could talk" would have hundreds of tales to tell about others, here and gone, who sat at the same place while they shared food, stories, tears, and laughter in her home. This is not the first interview that Kathleen has granted. I spoke with her in the early 1990s for my book, *Women of the Apache Nation,*[4] in which she was one of four contemporary Apache women who spoke extensively about their lives and their family history. Eighteen years later, much is similar but much is different.

Kathleen is a warm, welcoming, soft-spoken woman who looks younger than her advanced age of eighty plus years. She is one of those special people in a community who is widely known by a first name only. If someone on the reservation mentions "Kathleen," most everyone knows who they mean. Unfortunately, in 2006, right before Christmas, she was disabled by a fall in her home. She describes it humorously: "I did fine until I became eighty years old. Then all Hell broke loose." The fractured bones healed slowly and she now uses a walker to support her mobility, complaining all the time, not about her limits, but about causing inconveniences to relatives and friends who take her here and there.

Kathleen's late husband was Lee Kanseah, son of the boy Jasper who, in turn, was a horseholder to the warrior Yanosha. Kathleen still lives in the home where she and Lee raised two sons and other children. A grandson who works full time now lives with her, so she's on her own for the main part of the day. He cooks, cleans, and takes care of the house during his time off, but she putters around the kitchen and the rest of the three bedroom house in his absence. She also watches television and has become a football fan, although she won't disclose her favorite team. People come and go during the day, as periodically do the Community Health representatives who check on her medical condition; she is a diabetic. If no one is home, the visitors may simply wait on the porch for her, in comfortable chairs surrounding a large table, knowing that she will be back soon. Every now and then Kathleen talks about buying a car and getting back behind the wheel herself, but she knows that it's a pipe dream. Her driving skills have long been replaced by other qualities.

Church services at St. Joseph's Apache Mission, followed by lunch at a local restaurant with a friend or two, are her main Sunday excursions out of the house. Fellow churchgoers greet her cordially before and after the Mass when she sometimes stops at the parish hall for coffee and donuts. She often chides the people for not coming to visit her more than they do. The priest learned he is not immune from her rebukes.

Kathleen is a naturally happy woman with a good sense of humor and can find something amusing in most situations, with the exception of health care. Retired as a nurse after having worked with public health hospitals on Indian reservations around the country, her main concern in this interview is about the deteriorating health care at Mescalero. While working at the Mescalero hospital she helped many of the former prisoners of war when they were hospitalized with various medical conditions. Mention a name to her and she'll say, "Oooh, I remember him. I took care of him." She has somewhat forgiven—somewhat only—the United States for its imprisonment of her people, the Chiricahua Apaches; her father was born a prisoner of war. A photo of him as a boy in the POW camp at Fort Sill hangs on the dining room wall.

Mescalero has always been home to her, regardless of where she nursed or how long she was gone from the reservation. She can look back over a long life well lived, but she doesn't dwell in the past. As she holds the latest great-grandchild in her arms—there are at least a dozen or more—the joy in her face is unmistakable. She is an Apache woman whose bloodlines reach back into history and, without a doubt, will extend well into the future as do her hopes for the tribe.

Ed Little

Ed and I were around each other back in the early 1970s in Santa Fe but were never co-workers. He was part of the administration of what became the All Indian Pueblo Council and I worked for the Community Action programs. Our paths intersected periodically as we, each in our way, attempted to fill the goals of the Great Society programs that were popular at the time. Years passed with no contact but then we saw each other again as Marian Kelley and I were on the reservation interviewing Apaches for this book. Ed's sister, Sister Juanita Little (see interview below) suggested him as a speaker and we readily agreed. Happily for us, he responded quickly when we telephoned and asked for an interview—dropping his sister's name. We met shortly after that at the family home he shares with his sister when he is on the reservation. Ed sat at the head of a table.

Ed can appear intimidating at first. He's tall with a deep rich voice and definitely conveys the impression that he knows who he is as a Mescalero man and what he's all about. One immediately senses that he has held important authoritative positions both and in out of tribal confines. Simultaneously, he's friendly, gentle, and thoughtful as he expresses himself, and speaks with heartfelt sincerity about having the best interests of the tribal members at heart.

Our conversation with Ed lasted nearly three hours—the longest interview—during which only a few interruptions impeded the discussion. The house telephone and his cell phone rang several times, his son popped in for advice, we took a break, and his hearty laughter filled the room now and then. At the end of the interview, he seemed ready for more, and said he was pleased, as we were, with the results.

Ed left the reservation shortly afterward to drive the long distance to San Juan Pueblo (now called Ohkay Owingeh—his maternal ancestral home) for a visit with his wife and family, a trip he made almost every weekend when he was employed by the Mescalero tribe. He commented that he had planned to stay a while at San Juan but would be available by cell phone should we need to contact him regarding the interview. In consideration of our schedule, he estimated when he would return to Mescalero and would be able to meet again with us.

Ed's type is becoming a rarity—an educated man, experienced in the world of work beyond the reservation, but a traditional Apache living on the reservation who prefers many of the old customs to those of the modern, fast-paced world of the twenty-first century. It is easy to understand why. In his testimony he describes a crippling bout with rheumatoid arthritis as a young man in his twenties that Western scientific medicine could not help, even after months of hospitalization, but traditional medicine people cured him. As a modern Apache Ed simultaneously keeps traditions in his mind and envisions a business future for the tribe.

At the time of this interview, Ed was once again working for the tribe. Not wanting to use his family car for the day-to-day job-related activities that may require driving over rough terrain, he bought a truck. The truck is fire engine red.

Claudine Saenz

As a Warm Springs Apache woman with a distinguished heritage, Claudine represents both the old and the new on the reservation. Her bloodlines reach back into a time before the 1800s—the first documented history of her family—when the Apaches were free roaming and fulfilling what they believed to be their mandate from God. Chief Victorio[5] is her ancestor, as is Mangas Coloradas[6] and Martine, who was Geronimo's relative and the army scout who found him hiding in Mexico's Torres Mountains prior to his surrender. Her mother was the late Evelyn Martine Gaines, born a prisoner of war, and one of the last remaining survivors of the twenty-seven years of incarceration. Having been very close to her mother, Claudine knows the stories, knows the history behind the stories, and knows the lifeways behind the stories.

Ordinarily, she does not participate in interviews because of past episodes after which she was misquoted. Yet she feels she should at least be briefly consulted when words are being written about her ancestors. Recently, an author wrote about Victorio, putting together the circumstances and situations he experienced. "It reads like a novel," said Claudine. "Nobody talked to me about this."[7] She feels that outsiders' curiosity about her heritage often leads nowhere, nothing comes of it, and therefore she usually does not make herself available.

Our case was clearly different. Claudine has been our friend for years. We have shared many meals, laughs, and conversations together, especially during ceremonies and other times both on and off the reservation. For this interview, she invited us to her home where we spent a Sunday afternoon sitting around a small table enjoying one another's company. It certainly was a comfortable informal setting and one we have grown accustomed to over the years as we have been guests in many homes.

On another occasion, Marian Kelley and I sat beside Claudine on a cold weekend in March of 2007. We were outdoors at the Cochise Stronghold in Arizona's Chiricahua Mountains. By invitation from the Cochise family, we were attending a commemorative occasion—recognizing the significance of heritage through honoring Cochise in one of the places where he camped. As night fell and the Mountain Spirit Dancers appeared around the bonfire, our easy conversation ceased. We sat in companionable silence in that small group, each woman lost in her own thoughts, including my daughter and my young granddaughter who was wrapped in blankets, sleeping in my lap. It was not a new experience. For years we all have sat together, including Claudine's mother, at Mescalero during the annual July puberty ceremony. Now that Mrs. Gaines is no longer with us, we pull our aluminum chairs closer to fill her spot, but not too close, respecting the memory of a woman who was one of the most highly esteemed individuals on the reservation.

Claudine is close to the traditional expectation of an Apache woman. She thrives in the middle of her family—adult children and grandchildren—and needs very little social exposure to the outside world. If she goes anywhere, it's usually with a family member; Claudine drives. But as a professional woman—head of the Community Health Representative program—she is an R.N.—she guides her staff who delivers health care services to the needy. Her modest office is located in one of the reservation's vacated buildings—it once was an elementary school—and contains a desk, a computer, a telephone, and a photo of her mother on the wall. She had retired previously from her work at Mescalero's hospital but was asked in 2008 by the president of the tribe to come back to work. An intriguing fact about her: Claudine was a United States Marine.

Sister Juanita Little, OSF

This Mescalero Apache woman is a rock star in the reservation's St. Joseph's Apache Mission church. When she started her adult life as a member of the Franciscan Sisters of Our Lady of Perpetual Help, I'm certain she had no idea of who she would become years later in the eyes of her fellow tribal members—a nun who is truly beloved and revered both on and off the reservation. Young and old, regardless of religious affiliation, know her and stop to talk with her, whether at church, in a local restaurant, or in a shop or supermarket in nearby Ruidoso or Alamogordo. Tribal members' regard for her is especially obvious when, during Sunday Mass, Apaches returning from communion at the altar stop at her pew to hug her or whisper a few words. After the service she remains in the church for at least half an hour, accommodating parishioners who have something to speak with her about.

I first saw Sister Juanita about twenty years ago, in the mid-1980s, when a friend and I, visiting Kathleen Kanseah, were invited to Mass on a warm Sunday morning. As we sat quietly and waited for the service to start, a woman with a shock of snow-white hair, and dressed very fashionably, dashed past us and sat a few pews closer to the altar. It was obvious by her firm step and body language that she was someone of authority, someone who was sure of herself and knew her way around a church. Later I inquired and learned that this religious Sister, along with being a Mescalero Apache with family roots also in Ohkay Owingeh, was well known throughout the area.

Through the years since that first sighting I have come to know Sister Juanita as a respected teacher—she was once a Catholic school principal—an advocate for women's rights, a member of a family noted for its prestige within the tribe, and a matriarch in many ways within her family. Not incidentally, she is Ed Little's big sister.

I first interviewed Sister Juanita in 1993 for an earlier book.[8] At that time we faced each other while sitting on a bench in a small chapel within St. Joseph's Mission; a tape recorder was between us. When we recently reviewed that testimony, I asked if anything had changed. "I'm even firmer in those beliefs than I expressed back then," she said, telling me in so many words that she still knew her own mind.

This time around, we initially met with Sister in December of 2007 at the Mescalero school, where she was working; she was one of our first speakers. To arrange the interview, I had previously telephoned her, renewed our acquaintance, and described the book I was planning. We discussed the premises and I asked permission to have another conversation. She agreed and we set the date and time. After that interview concluded, we realized that there was more to be said, so a second discussion came about a few months later. Even though we are now officially "done," I have a feeling there is still more to be said, more to be elaborated upon, more topics to be explored.

Sister Juanita is organized, comes prepared to talk, and brings supporting documentation to the meeting. For example, in talking about her efforts to cause changes in one area of her working experience, she handed over letters she had written to authority figures in support of her point. They ignored her at their peril—one of her personality traits is persistence and she doesn't give up easily.

These days Sister, age seventy-four at the time of the interviews, still works full time, doing whatever the school's administration officials ask of her. She functions mainly as a liaison with parents; she also counsels, a position that requires making home visits and transporting students to off reservation distant facilities when necessary. She was recently asked for her comments on the design of an innovative truancy ordinance, and she is professionally involved in creating a foster care program on the reservation.

At St. Joseph's Apache Mission she participates as a Eucharistic Minister, teaches confirmation classes, and presents the Apache community—Catholic and Protestant—with a role model—a high quality, flesh and blood symbol of Christianity in the modern age. She effectively juggles her life in the church with services to the tribe as she walks her talk in whatever she does.

The Warriors

Joey Padilla

With his unique perspective as a medicine man, Joey Padilla adds a dimension to this book that otherwise could not be included. Readers might be surprised at some of his thoughts but must keep in mind that Apache medicine people see the life around them differently than do others. They view things through a lens that is heavily spiritual, and often times with only a small dose of what passes for reality among friends, relatives, and non-Indians. So, while some of his comments may seem unusual, they are not to those of all backgrounds who understand the Apache culture. His participation in this project was an extraordinary experience, and we deeply appreciate his willingness to talk with us, have his comments published, and to be photographed. Many of his points of view were known to us as his friends but had not been expressed publicly in the past.

To begin the interview, we drove high up the mountain to Cow Camp No. 1, where he was employed as the cook for about twenty wranglers and cow men in charge of the tribe's herd.[9] We took Kathleen Kanseah with us; she had asked to come along and we couldn't say no. When Joey saw our vehicle drive up to the complex of ranch buildings, he came out of the "mess hall" to greet us, a big smile on his face, accompanied by his faithful dog, Cowgirl, ambling behind him. He took us into a large one-room building with long tables and benches, no chairs, all the while describing the surroundings and the nutritious meals he prepares three times daily for the cowboys. At the far end of the room was a kitchen, his pride. After showing off his working space, he directed us to the table and we sat across from him, starting our conversation.

At times the manager of the cow camp came into the mess hall and joined the discussion, agreeing with Joey about this and that, or enhancing Joey's last comment. Two men talking at once, each bouncing ideas and experiences off the other, was a bit disconcerting but we didn't interrupt. Every now and then Kathleen, seated on the far end of the table, also put her thoughts into the discussion. Thus, at times it became somewhat of a round table talk rather than an interview, but that seemed fine with Joey, and so it was with us.

At the end of our conversation Joey retreated into the kitchen to peel potatoes for the evening meal, still chatting about life at the cow camp and the innovations he hoped to implement. Afterward, he accompanied us to our car and bid us a fond goodbye as we hooked our seatbelts and made ready to travel back down the mountain.

It may seem strange to some readers that a medicine man can also be a cook or have another occupation as well, but keep in mind that medicine people—men and women—deal with spiritual issues on a daily basis. What can be more spiritual than nourishing body and soul with food to keep the spirit alive?

Depree Shadowwalker

This talented Apache woman has expertise in many areas—home remodeling, architecture, design, linguistics, computer sciences. Having already acquired a master's degree, she is in the process now of completing the requirements for a Ph.D., an educational effort that requires her to commute weekly from Mescalero to the University of Arizona in Tucson, a drive of about ten hours each way; her commitment ought to be an example to others.

She wasn't always named Depree Shadowwalker. For years before she was known reservation-wide as Debbie Smith. She explains, in her interview, her reasons for changing her name even though most everyone still calls her Debbie Smith. She lives a goodly distance away from the center of the reservation in a wooded area surrounded by pine trees. Her 2008 Christmas card, which she e-mailed, was a photo of that special place decorated with the first snowfall of the season.

She has a connection to the earth and discusses it in her interview, telling readers, for example, that the reservation has smells she needs to sustain herself. Silently referenced by her at this moment is the historical Apache relationship with the earth, a relationship that extends to the time before time and is evoked simply by an aroma. In this regard, Depree personifies the ages-old Apache spiritual unity with the earth.[10]

But, she often does not exhibit the usual behavioral patterns of historical Apache women.[11] Thoroughly modern Depree is outspoken and thus controversial, a trait she believes has hampered her success as a professional within the tribe. Also differing from orthodoxy and adding to the raised-eyebrow view of her by some Apaches is the vehicle she drives: a big, black truck with high rollover bars, certainly unlike the preferred image of an Apache woman, even in the twenty-first century. Nonetheless, Depree still exhibits some of the customary traits: she is involved with her family, she has respect for the elders, and she is concerned about the children and the future of the tribe.

We sat down with Depree in our motel room during one of our monthly trips from southern Arizona for interviews on the reservation. She arrived carrying bags of fast food for our lunch, but Marian and I had already eaten. So, while she enjoyed the food we chatted about this and that, telling her that after our conversation we wanted to take a photo of her to accompany the interview. She demurred, saying her hair was not stylish that day but would return with her own photo, one that she would prefer to be published.

At the conclusion of our discussion we were struck by the candid way in which Depree expressed herself and her stated unhappiness with the way events on the reservation were unfolding. Yet at the end of a long list of problems, she promised that if anyone would try to take the reservation away, they would have to have a fight with her. That would be quite a challenge for anyone.

Alfred LaPaz

Catch him if you can. That was our task after the interview with Alfred was transcribed and ready for his review. After many unsuccessful attempts at contacting him, we concluded that Alfred had become invisible. He was nowhere to be seen, didn't respond to telephone calls, and didn't answer notes placed in his mailbox at tribal headquarters (he was a member of the Tribal Council). But if something serious had happened, we believed someone would have told us. Still . . . We learned later that suddenly, as life sometimes happens, Alfred had become extremely busy, so occupied with tribal business and family circumstances—he is a strong family man—that his cell phone rang incessantly and he had very little time for anything other than what was immediate. When we did eventually meet up with him, he apologized profusely, just as he answered another call or two.

In conversation, Alfred is a careful speaker, conscientious, deliberately choosing his words so that there will be no mistake. He is a polished gentleman who smiles frequently, especially when mentioning his family; his sincerity in that regard is certainly unmistakable. When editing his transcript for the first time, he was taken aback, found it hard to believe he had said so much, and wanted to change some of it to more accurately reflect his opinions. Thus began a review that required three separate occasions during which he took great care to make certain each of the words he selected conveyed the exact meaning he intended. Once he lost track of the hour, and when reminded he abruptly dropped his pen and dashed out the front door—late for a Tribal Council meeting more than thirty minutes away. I thought it would be days before I saw him again, but I was surprised. He telephoned for another appointment soon afterward and he completed his first review. After I retyped the interview and incorporated his changes, we began the process anew until at long last the words you read carefully depict this Mescalero Apache man—the unique individual that he wants you to know.

Debi Martinez

A Chiricahua Apache descendant of the great Cochise, as a tribal judge she is also a leader. Debi is unafraid to speak her mind, to level accusations, or to express herself as she believes is necessary to identify the causes of intolerable situations on her beloved reservation. In a quiet way. On a daily basis she encounters the consequences of the terrible addictions and dysfunctions that plague many of the people on the Mescalero reservation today, the causes of which she frankly attributes to the unavoidable contagious influences of white society and historical trauma. Perhaps that is why her eyes are sad, why her smile is slow in coming. Perhaps she speaks so softly to hide the scream that would erupt if she really let go of her emotions.

It is difficult to contact Debi during the day unless one is prepared to sit in the tribal court's lobby and catch her between cases, as I did on one unforgettable day. Within an hour's time, at least one dozen Apaches—mostly young people—filed in and out. Some were awaiting pieces of official paper, some were there for hearings, and some were friends. Occasionally an older person came in the door, looked around, identified the friend or relative, and left. An air of seriousness permeated the air, and while chatting with each other no one laughed, no one smirked, and very few smiled. The atmosphere was glum. Debi remained behind closed doors, conducting the business of the day until 4:30 in the afternoon, when the doors were closed and she and two other judges left; her husband, Jerry, was waiting for her.

Jerry is of Mayan descent. He and Debi are also vendors, selling South American and Latin American wares, including jewelry, tapestries, cloths of many colors, handbags, and other colorful goods. When they are together in these settings, Debi may sit behind a table with a grandchild on her lap, or cross the room to greet a friend, or chat with passers-by, many of whom are non-Indian customers and do not realize the woman in front of them carries the blood of a famous American hero. Even though her mother, Elbys Naiche Hugar, is somewhat of a celebrity among outsiders, Debi remains content to live her life behind the scenes, quietly going about her daily routine. She is both an observer and an active participant in tribal life these days, always ready to speak her mind. But, she doesn't volunteer to do so; she has to be asked.

When we first approached her regarding an interview, she jumped at the chance to express herself. Faithful to her word, months later she sat at our kitchen table for hours, both during and after the interview. Cochise would be proud of her candor and forthright attitude.

Larry Shay

An artist. A poet. A philosopher. These and other descriptions cannot paint a complete picture of this kind man whom readers would fully appreciate. He is quiet, even contemplative, during the middle of conversations both on and off the record. One senses that Larry has been disappointed many times during his lifetime; he doesn't laugh easily.

We met Larry in the Tribal Council chambers and sat with him for more than an hour, listening intently and caught up in his responses to our questions; he measures each word. He is proud to be an Apache, proud to live on the reservation, and, if reincarnation is possible, would want to come back to the reservation as yet another Apache.

He is a drummer and can spend a lot of time sitting on a bench simply singing and drumming. It is as if he is lost in the steady beat—the heartbeat of the earth, the heartbeat of his people. Stopping for water, he may look around at his audience and, surprised, will rise to greet each one individually.

Larry is also a student of Apache history. During one conversation about when the ancestors crossed the Bering Strait in their migration from Mongolia to the Arctic Circle, he paused to find the correct words and then said he didn't believe they did. How so, we asked. "I think we have always been here," he said, a serious look in his eyes. So much for the evidence, the historians, the anthropologists, the archaeologists, and others. One cannot quarrel with his answer and one would not want to do so in any case. It might offend Larry and no one would want to deliberately, or even inadvertently, hurt him.

Larry calls himself the "war chief" of the tribe, somewhat of a switch in personalities. If he were indeed such a figure in historical times, wars would have been infrequent, and when occurring, easily resolved with his irresistible smile and peaceful demeanor.

The Horseholders

Eliza Yuzos

Eliza, whose nickname is Gussie, can usually be seen surrounded by young children—four of her own and others of her family. Occasionally she and her kids are all crowded together in the front seat of an old truck she drives; the youngest one sits on the eldest one's lap. Always ready with a big smile, Gussie reminds me of a traditional Chiricahua Apache woman—deeply involved with loved ones. "They teach me Apache," she said, describing the moment in her day when the kids come home from school and practice what they learned in their language class. She and her husband, Jay, with the children in tow, visit her grandmother often, sometimes sweeping the porch when too much debris accumulates because of swirling wind, or tidying up here and there indoors. On holidays, Gussie and Jay can be found in Grandma's kitchen, cooking a special meal for an unknown number of people who may arrive to help celebrate. And eat. Always ready to greet everyone with a big smile, she handles herself with a look backward to historical times when an Apache woman's purpose was to carry on the culture through her children. Yes, she is young but older in many ways than her years.

Dan Kanseah Jr.

This young man has held down the same job with the tribe for about ten years. He works at the Inn of the Mountain Gods Resort in the Ski

Apache shop during the winters and in the Pro Golf shop during the summers. He is companionable, a good conversationalist, and a football fan; a large TV screen occupies one corner of the living room in the house he shares with his grandmother. Having no vehicle of his own, he is also a scrambler, hustling around on his days off to get a ride to Ruidoso, where he shops for the house and for his dog, Bam Bam, and the cat Yah-te-hey. He chops wood in the winter to fill the potbellied stove in the living room and makes certain, before he leaves for work, that his grandmother has enough wood stacked up near the stove to get her through the cold days.

Like many Apaches, including his late father, he is a very good artist, but he doesn't draw much these days. He is the only male in a family of sisters who have children of their own and takes his position seriously, especially with his young nephews whom he lets "sleep over" with him in his bedroom. He wants to be a role model for them. Dan is a good cook, as one can tell by opening the door of the new stainless steel refrigerator he bought his grandmother.

If Danny had lived in historical times, he would have been an exemplary horseholder, looking carefully after his mentor's well being, taking care of things around the camp, and making certain that every need was met.

Kiana Mangas

As a young woman, we expected Kiana to be more contemporary than she is. We anticipated that she would be as vivacious and full of life as any sixteen-year-old would be, but we were surprised. She is polite, quite self-contained, very aware of her family's history, articulate in describing the teenage life around her, and indeed comfortable with her absence from it. As a serious young woman, she doesn't participate in the girls/boys environment, preferring to have only one friend with whom she shares laughter. Kiana is remarkably traditional in her beliefs, and puts her trust in Ussen (Apache Creator) for her future, although she plans on a career in art or the culinary arts. Her ancestors were famous tribal leaders in historical times, including Lozen, who has been described in literature and on film as the famous "warrior woman." Kiana shows the same spiritual depth that Lozen must have had—an unshakeable belief that Ussen has His eye on the Apache people and will keep them safe and thriving far into the future.

Conversations

THE ELDERS

TESTIMONY OF KATHLEEN KANSEAH

I am Kathleen Kanseah, age eighty-one, Chiricahua Apache. My mother's name was Martina Little Smith; she had a Spanish grandmother. My father's name was Hopkins Smith Sr., and my brother's name was Hopkins Smith Jr. He was the oldest of the boys. I was the only girl and I was the eldest child. My brother Hopkins was in the Navy. Edward was my second brother and he was in the Air Force. My third brother was in the Navy and then the last brother, who is still alive, didn't join the service.

My father was born in Oklahoma[1] but was raised here on the reservation. My grandmother, Gertrude Smith, on my father's side was a full blood Chiricahua Apache. Dad was in the service for two years in Fort Bliss [Texas] and some tell me I was born in Fort Bliss and some tell me I was born on the reservation. The pictures I have seen of Dad holding me as a little girl and Mom standing beside him in front of a tent look like the reservation. They didn't have homes. They just lived in tents. Not a tipi. It was almost like an army tent but it was white. It was just one room; you can't divide a tent. They had two big double beds in there; we used baskets for our clothes and cooked in an arbor.

Mom and Dad got married in Fort Bliss because he was in the service for two years. When he got out they moved here to Mescalero. He was working at the forestry and he did some carpentry. Dad was also a policeman for many years. When Mom married Dad she was working at the hospital. She was a cook.

Where did you live on the reservation? Where the Dutch Reformed Church is today. We lived in two tents facing each other with an arbor in the middle. We slept in one and the other one was where we ate in the winter. We spent the summer months in the arbor. Then Dad built a small house and we all slept in one room. And then my step-grandfather built a house. Everybody lived in tents. I was real close to my grandmother. They had a place out in Carrizo.[2] We used to go out there to visit them and then Grandma wanted me to stay with her. We'd get on a horse and ride up the canyon toward White Mountain together. My brothers had horses and we used to ride up to Head Springs and sometimes we used to ride over the mountain to Nogal and then ride the reservation fence line all the way back to the house. It didn't seem far at that time but now you go clear around the reservation to get there.

How old were you when you got married? I was about twenty-two years old. My husband's name was Lee Kanseah. His father, Jasper, was a prisoner of war in Florida, Alabama, and Fort Sill.[3] And then he came to Whitetail on the reservation. My father-in-law is the youngest warrior sitting with Geronimo in the famous picture in front of the train. *How many children did you have?* Just two boys. One passed away a few years ago.

Tell me how your nursing career began. When I was in high school they needed somebody to help with the records at the old Indian hospital, so I used to go in there and help [with] filing records. Then they told me to work in the clinic, to see who was next in line to go in to see the doctor there. Like a receptionist, I had to sit there and tell them to go in. I got interested in it.

I was a nurse for twenty-nine years. I worked in Minnesota when I got out of school and they were going to transfer me to Washington State to the TB hospital but I was there only three days when they closed the place. I then went back to Minnesota and afterward was transferred to the Navajo country.[4] I came back to the reservation, worked about a year here and went to Santa Fe. I liked being a nurse. We used to have to mix our own medicines—the liquids and the powder both.

Did someone teach you some of the old medicines? My grandmother Gertrude Smith did. I used to go on horseback up toward White Mountain with her. She taught me all those different medicines. I helped her pick them, put them in individual sacks, and then put them all in a big sack. But up to today I don't remember any of those medicines. My Dad used to say, "You'll never remember those because it wasn't meant for you." *Was your grandmother a medicine woman?* No, she just used to pick the medicines and used it just for the immediate family and the widespread family. Nobody else. She wasn't a medicine woman the way the white man says it.

Will you describe the health care situation on the reservation today? Instead of having three or four doctors [we need] permanent doctors, not every three or four months changing—that's why I left the hospital here. They're always in training, they're not doctors yet. After three or four months, other doctors come in; maybe one will be permanent for about a year. They don't like it and they leave. That's why I quit going. In the old days the doctors stayed.

[In answer to your question], I don't think the government is killing Apaches through bad health care. But it depends on the person. If the doctor orders medicine for them, some of them don't understand how to take it. Some might say, "Well, they told me to take this three times a day, but I'll take it all and that's it."

If the tribe would be in complete charge of the reservation's hospital and had the proper resources from the U.S. government, would the tribe do a better job in running the hospital? No because the tribe doesn't have the educated people to run the hospital, so if the government turns it over to the tribe it will be a great loss. And another thing, most of the staff works for Public Health and some of them are all right and some of them are not.

The other day you mentioned the loss of the practice of traditional medicine. Tell me again, please. With the younger generation, the prayers, the healing, the medicine, is lost. You can tell they don't understand. So then the medicine man tells them in English but it doesn't come out the same. *By praying in English, is a prayer less powerful?* It doesn't come across in English. Like those girls in the big tipi during the puberty ceremony,[5] some don't understand the Indian language. And they just stand there dancing back and forth to the rhythm of the drum. But that drum and the songs mean a lot. The medicine men can feel it. If I have a relative in the big tipi, someone puts a chair there for me and I go and sit and look at the girls. They are dancing but they don't know what they are dancing about. It's sad.

Will the puberty ceremony eventually be lost? I don't think so. But some of the girls are already lost because they don't understand what's going on. They don't understand the songs. They don't understand the Indian language at all. The girls who understand the Indian language, it's different for them. The ones who don't understand the language at all, when they dance you see them looking around at the people standing in the tipi, and I can tell. Sometimes I sit there in my chair and I can just feel it. You can just feel the difference in the girls. Their behavior goes right along with it.

Isn't the puberty ceremony the heart of the tribe? It is. The way I think about it is that if they keep having it at the feast grounds [a public place] where there's so much distraction,[6] I think they'll lose it. Those girls who have feasts way out at Whitetail or wherever the family wants to have it privately, I think it will last. Someone told me that when the girls dance they are supposed to be listening to the songs that are being sung. Even if they have distraction they should concentrate and listen carefully to the songs. I think those songs are just beautiful. *Are the sacred songs in danger of being lost?* No. So far they haven't been but a lot of the people in their thirties and forties are losing the songs. You can see it sometimes when they are dancing out there. When you are dancing you have to watch that fire. I don't know if you noticed some of the older ones looking at that fire. When they are singing there's a lot of things in those songs that will tell you about the tribe. Sometimes you can see things in the fire. It depends on the person. Right now one of my grandchildren likes to dance out there and I always tell her to watch the fire. It will tell her a lot.

Some of the medicine men are young, just starting. One is my little cousin. His mom is my first cousin. He goes in there with his uncle or his dad, sits there, and listens. Some of them say you can just feel "the man upstairs" when they are singing. You have to really concentrate. There's a lot of distraction in the back.

I was tickled when your great-grandchildren sang in Apache and counted up to twenty. Do you see hope in them? Yes, I really do because my great-grandson has a little drum and he sits with the singers. He likes that. Now that he's learning the language, he's more into it. He can sing the songs but then right away he's distracted, puts his drum down, and goes out and plays. He's nine or ten years old.

With or without distraction, in five or ten years will the puberty ceremony still occur? I think it will.

Speaking of the possibility of losing some aspects of your culture, please tell me about your ancestral religion. It's not going to be lost. The late Eugene Chihuahua's[7] songs were very strong for the fire dancers[8] and you could feel it, especially when you were dancing. After he passed away I didn't dance for two years. When I started dancing again I felt good about it because he left the songs for us. But now I let it go because I can't dance.

And the language. Do you see hope for the language surviving, or is it dying? I don't see it dying. And I don't see the songs being lost. The medicine man who was sitting beside me yesterday knows all the songs and that boy that was sitting on the other side is the one who does a lot of that with his dad. He's about seventeen years old. There's hope with him. I saw this with my own eyes and I felt real good about it: a girl who had a feast [puberty ceremony] in the country hired him and he talked to her, telling her why he was doing this and that and he would ask her if she understood. He told her everything in Indian and I don't think she understood some of it so he'd ask her in English, "Do you know what I'm saying?" She'd slowly say "no," so he said, "Tell me how you're feeling, what you think about what I was saying. If you don't understand, tell me." So she came out and told him that she didn't understand part of what he was telling her. He explained it to her in English.

Tell me about education on the reservation today. One thing I like is that they're teaching the kids our language. My grandkids come in here and say something to me in Apache and I look at them. I ask, "What did you say?" One of them is kind of tongue-tied but she tries. She slowly told me what she said. Now that they have the new school, [the education] is all right. *It sounds like some changes have been made.* Yes. They've got all the kids up there. They're not down here where they can wander off. They're all up in one place on top of the hill and they have all kinds of things for them. It's just nice up there. About two weeks ago they had a program in which everything was in the Apache language. All the kids talked in Apache and they all sang in Apache. They were dressed like Apaches. It made me feel so good to see the kids up there. The kids here talk Apache, not fluently, but if you talk with them they look at you and wonder, "What did she say?" Or if they say something to me, they look at me and I say, "What did you say?" Then they shy away a little bit and I ask them again in Apache and then they'll come out and finally tell me. But you have to listen closely to them because they can't quite pronounce some of the words.

Tell me about your education. Did you go to boarding school? I wanted to go to the Santa Fe Indian School and so did my brother. So they let us go for one year. Then Mom and Dad took us out of there for some reason. I didn't want to go back for the second year. They were letting the Apache kids go to public school in Tularosa,[9] so we went to high school there.

And then I went to boarding school when they had one right here on the reservation. It was across the street from the Care Center. Up on the hill was one girls' building and one boys' building. In the middle was the dining room. The girls went first into the dining room to eat. We all sat on one side. Then the boys would come in from the other side and sit opposite. It was the same in Santa Fe.

What are your memories of Whitetail, where the former Apache prisoners, including your father, lived? I was very young. I vaguely remember my dad and mom had a little cabin up on a hillside when I was about two or three years old. They didn't live there; we used to go up there because my grandmother used to live somewhere close by. All of a sudden some of the people in the cabin ran out the door and I couldn't imagine what was going on. My Uncle Willis was a very tall man and he grabbed me and set me up on his shoulders. I didn't know why. He hung onto my arms and legs and as long as I was with him I felt all right. I didn't know why we were running but I enjoyed sitting on his shoulders. He ran up the hill with me and when he saw a low-hanging branch, he'd tell me to put my head down. They were chasing a skunk that was completely white. They'd never seen a white skunk before and it's a good thing it didn't turn around to spray them.

Tell me about a major event in your life. The atomic bomb. When they blasted the first atomic bomb out there at White Sands[10] I was walking from the house up to the tribal store and I heard that big explosion. The wind came real hard and I didn't know what was going on, so I ran up to the tribal store. I got in there and Mr. Prude said, "Well, they did it, they did it." That was all I could hear him say but I didn't know what they did. I asked Mr. Prude what in the world they were doing. I thought maybe the tribe was doing something down by the reservation line. He said, "No, it was a big explosion down at Holloman [Air Force Base]." And I didn't ask any more questions. Later on in high school I found out and wondered if anybody got hurt with all the radiation from that. I felt that hard wind but I never got anything from it.

Did the government inform the people that they were going to test the bomb? They might have. I don't know. When Mom and Dad were talking about it Dad asked, "Do you kids feel all right?" I asked why and then Dad explained it to us. I didn't feel anything but that air.

What was living on the reservation like during World War II? A lot of the men were going to war. All three brothers went to war. They all came back safely. Four of us girls went to Holloman Air Force Base to enlist and we were all standing in line. I don't know how my dad found out but he grabbed my arm and said, "Hey, girl, let's go." He took me out of that line and brought me home. When we were coming home I said, "Dad, I was going to join the Air Force." He said, "You don't have to go. You already have two brothers gone. Why do you have to go?" My oldest brother and the next one were gone. One was in the Navy and the other one in the Air Force. Then my youngest brother at that time went into the Navy too. Three of them were in the service already. Even Dad was in the Army stationed at Fort Bliss, but that was before the war.

Do you have a view of the tribe's future? I think about that sometimes and I think this younger generation doesn't understand the language at all and things get lost and lost. One day my brother and I were talking about it. He sings with the medicine men and I asked him about it. He said that at the rate it's going now, it might not last very long. That's how I feel about it. Maybe we might lose it in ten years—the girls, the dancing, the tipi.[11]

To me, it depends on the president [of the tribe]. These last presidents didn't show me any improvement in anything but education. They weren't doing anything for the elders. And now, this new president has been around.[12] He's a powerful man so when I heard him talking in our language, I agreed with a lot of things he said. It made me feel good inside. My personal feeling is that we were just on the verge of losing the tribe. Losing the whole reservation. This man who we have now has strong feelings about the tribe, and I'm glad that he went all over and got educated about a lot of things. Ph.D. Just look at all the guests that were at his inauguration. The new president is strong. I just felt so good about him. I shook his hand. He said, "Kathleen, I have to talk to you about something." I know what it is. When I was a tribal judge here he went into court and I don't remember what he went in there for but I shut him up right away and he went out. Found him not guilty. I guess he remembers that. But I didn't say anything now. I thought I'd wait until he was in office for a while and go through all the things that have to be done.

After he spoke up there's going to be a lot of hope for the future because he sees a lot of things that could be done. This president is a [descendant of] Cochise and he's strong. His education is what makes him strong. We need somebody like him. Now my people are very strong and they'll fight back in a reasonable way with a strong leader. I haven't had this kind of a discussion in a long time.

—January 12, 2008

TESTIMONY OF EDWARD LITTLE

I'm Edward Michael Little, a tribal member of the Mescalero Apache Tribe. I was born in 1941 and raised here in Mescalero. I'm sixty-six years old and I have lived a good part of my life here on the reservation. I was off the reservation for quite some time as well. Back in those days it was almost a must, there was almost no place to work. Work was pretty scarce. I lived here at Mescalero during my younger years. I left the reservation to go off to school.

There's a long story to my family's background. We were actually adopted. There's a question as to whether we were Mexican or possibly Lipan Indian. We were actually fighting with the Chiricahua and so they [the Mexicans] ran all the Apaches out of Mexico at one time. Therefore, they came this way. My grandpa, Andy Little, was running around the street and someone came by and picked him up, brought him to Mescalero.

Names were given many times by the soldiers. He was a little guy, so they named him "Little." A lot of our tribal people are named like that. For example, Big Mouth had a big mouth. Cross Eyes. Sombrero. That's how the names came down.

My grandpa was handed around to different families who would take care of him. When he came of age they told him to go back and see if he could trace any of his people in Mexico. He was welcome to stay or come back. So, he went to Mexico and apparently he didn't like it, or wasn't used to it. So he came back and he stayed here. He was quite a figure among the tribe here. Like a chief in a way. He died when he was about one hundred years old.

There's a lot of stories about my ancestors, my grandpa mainly. One story goes that one time during the Depression when they weren't getting any rations, or wheat was scarce, my grandpa had plenty of water and so he used to raise different crops here. He had wheat, corn, all kinds of vegetables. Plus he had a lot of sheep. So he asked the people to help him and told them they could take what they wanted. My uncle said camps were all around here and the people stayed here. They would plant and harvest. My grandpa helped the people survive during the Depression when there was no food.

Your education? I went to elementary school here in Mescalero. Afterward was boarding school. We used to have the basics here until the sixth grade. And then we were sent to boarding school; for us it was generally in Albuquerque. I went to the Albuquerque Indian School. Some parents who could afford it would send you to Catholic school, like St. Catherine's in Santa Fe or different Catholic boarding schools. I stayed there in Albuquerque the whole school year. Came back in the summer. Most of the time we'd come home for Christmas. But usually we stayed there from the time we started until summer. I was there through the seventh, eighth, and ninth grades. I thought it was a good experience. I did all right in boarding school.

But at that time they decided to integrate into the public school system. That was about 1954. Then I started school in Tularosa. The high school was the only school available to us. Ruidoso was too far. Not too many people lived on that side then. Most people lived here [closer to Tularosa], so we all went to Tularosa. That's when they started it and we didn't have to go to boarding school anymore. I went as far as high school. I never did get a degree. I had an opportunity but didn't work toward a degree.

Describe your work history, please. I have had a lot of different kinds of experiences here on the reservation. I worked at Cow Camp, spent several summers out there, when I was about fifteen years old. At that time we as a tribe had about seven thousand head of cattle. We had individual brands so we had to pretty much fend for ourselves as a family to make sure our brands were kept up. That's the main reason why I was sent out to Cow Camp—to look after my family's herd. Almost every family who had any cattle would do that. You'd be out there at Cow Camp watching your family's interest. Then they changed it and we went into a single association on brands. After that there wasn't a need then to send our kids out to Cow Camp to protect our interests because it turned into shares. Then we became stockholders. They took how many cattle you had and turned them into shares. Some had more shares than others. You could bid on them but you could also buy them from somebody else. For me, learning to be a cowboy was a heck of an experience. It turns you into a man pretty young.

Not too long after that we were into a lot of firefighting. I went to quite a few fires. We called them the Red Hats, which I guess was the forerunner of Hot Shots that are out there now. We kind of became an elite group. One summer when I was about seventeen years old, we went all summer. There was no break for about twenty days. Those were some of my early work experiences. I did a lot of farming during that time, too. My brother raised a lot of things—alfalfa, apples, things like that. I had to do a lot of that kind of work because I was asked to. We had our own milking cows. My dad bought two Jerseys and a Guernsey. My mother used to sell milk to everyone in the valley around here. I had to get up early in the morning and milk those cows. You'd be surprised how much milk I got. In the morning I'd get maybe close to fifty gallons of milk.

During high school my dad contracted with the BIA to fix all their equipment and take care of their equipment, so they had a big garage. We did that for a few years, a lot of mechanics and things like that. The government couldn't pay their bill on time and my dad just couldn't continue to afford to care for their equipment.

Back in those days, and it still carries over to some extent that I've seen, there was no encouragement for private enterprise on this reservation. It was even worse when Wendell Chino[1] was here because he didn't care for it at all. If you did want to do it, the first thing he would bring up, was that according to our tribal code, you cannot be in competition with another tribal enterprise. If it was a service station, you can't do that. That was hard. A lot of people were held back who wanted to get into business. It was discouraging. And then there were no resources to help someone get into business, so that made it harder. No incentive to do it, either.

My dad was one of the few who were in business. He was in the logging business way prior to that so I got a taste of logging with him as well. He was a logging contractor. I was not that big at the time when I helped him do some logging around here. Back in the early days he was a plumbing contractor during the war. He was exempt from going to the war because his product was needed. So he got deferred. What really killed him were tires. He could not get decent tires. They gave him all the old tires and the military took the rest. He said he spent all his time fixing tires on the truck.

Is logging on the reservation productive today? It's not good at all. Nationwide and statewide there's not one. We are the only logging operation open in the whole state right now. I don't know how we have survived. We don't have quality timber on our reservation anymore. We could not even supply ourselves if we had to. It's operational, but the tribe is subsidizing it. That's the thing I couldn't deal with anymore. No income coming in from any of our logging operations at all.

Is Cow Camp producing any income? Not really. We've had a couple of hits. If you can sell about three hundred to four hundred head of cattle you are going to receive couple hundred thousand dollars, which is good money. But to run an operation like that, it's nothing. It's already gone for feed. That's why our cattle operation just went down the tubes from what it used to be. And there was poor management over the years. The BIA never managed our resources well. We lost a lot of water. Without water in the mountains you can't graze the cattle.

Tell me about your experiences as a Ford Foundation fellow.[2] There was a year-long leadership development scholarship that they gave. You had to apply. Mostly they gave it to teachers and people in educational departments but then there was also such a thing as community development. They started looking into rural communities. That was the first time they looked at the tribes as a community, as a small town. Their quota was less than fifty thousand people. Over that they wouldn't look at. They came and recruited and told me that I was overqualified. That made me mad. I had been told that in the past. "You are overqualified." What did they mean? I went and argued with the guy and they ended up giving me a fellowship. That was quite an experience. I really enjoyed that. It opened my eyes to the fact that there was another world. This was in 1968–69. There was a lot of stuff going on. I happened to go with other people from Mescalero—Paul Ortega, Fred Peso. We were the first ones on that fellowship. About a year afterward, Carleton went.[3]

As a Ford fellow, you could set your own curriculum. They worked with you regarding what your interests were, the political, or this and that. We traveled. They want you to travel and have different experiences, see different things. Leadership. I elected to go to the New Mexico Commission on Indian Affairs. They called it "interning." So I interned for about a year. The director told me, "Ed, you should move on. I'm not teaching you anything." That was in Santa Fe. John Ranier, his name was. He was a good man. I wanted to intern with him.

At the time, the National Congress of American Indians[4] was having their conference in Albuquerque. The guy that ran the program for us asked me if I'd like to help—work with that conference, set it up, and all that. So I did. That was another good experience. From there I was able to make more connections with people from the National Congress and other tribes. Then I moved to Washington D.C. to do an internship for three months there with the Bureau of Indian Affairs[5] to start with. I was fortunate because the commissioner, Louie Bruce, had a young man as his executive assistant. This man's father died and he was leaving. So Mr. Bruce asked me to take his place. I learned a lot. Oh, that was great. It fell into my lap, including a real coveted parking spot. Everybody was mad at me because I got the parking spot that went along with that position. At the time the Bureau of Indian Affairs had its own building. I stayed with Louie Bruce almost two months and then the other guy came back. So then I moved on.

I interned with another guy by the name of Morrie Thompson. He was the assistant secretary for Indian Affairs. They had just created that position and so I was fortunate to intern with him, too. It exposed me to a lot of commission hearings. Morrie asked me to tell him about different tribes, bills and things that they were trying to get through. That was interesting.

But I was unable to come back to Mescalero. When I ended my stint, the one year with the Ford Foundation, they hired me to work for them. I worked for them for almost three years. That was another experience. I was at a field office with Ford-funded operations in Albuquerque. We gave twenty fellowships a year. So they asked me to run a post fellowship operation. What I would do is go into the communities where we sent people back after their fellowship. Some of them fit right back into the community; some of them had a hard time. Like me. I just couldn't fit back in here. It wasn't that easy to get back in here. There were no jobs available and all that experience that I had gotten didn't do me much good here.

The tribe had no place, no position for you? At the time they didn't. I came and visited with Mr. Chino. He was real supportive and acknowledged us whenever he could—what we did. But the advice he gave me was, "Ed, I know you can get a job out there. It's easy enough. What I think would be the best thing for you is if you would get out there and get as much experience as you can. Then you can come back and you have something to offer your community." That's what he told me. He also said, "Right now, even if you came back, I wouldn't know what to do."

But you had all that experience to offer the tribe. Yes, and more. Prior to that, right before the Ford fellowship, I wound up in a good position. I had run the roads program for the tribe. I became the branch chief of roads for the BIA on the reservation. I was only about twenty-six years old. At that time, instead of the government giving a contract to somebody, they would provide us, the tribe, with the money and we would build the roads. I was a mechanic during that time and an operator. As we went along I gained a lot of experience and I was taking some correspondence courses. I took one for a highway engineer. So it worked out real good. I did a lot of studying, sent it in and that worked pretty good. I was able to get an associate's degree in highway engineering. That's how I got on to run the program.

With all of this happening, have you had any military experience? No. I didn't have to go to the military. I was on deferred retirement because I was married and was with the Ford Foundation as an employee and the fellowship.

As a Native American during that time, did you encounter any discrimination? Well, I saw it different places. Probably at sometime it was worse here, like in Ruidoso. It was pretty bad there. If you went into a restaurant you couldn't eat. That was in the late 1940s, into the 1950s. I remember when I about five or six years old and went to some of those restaurants, the owners would come out and tell you that they couldn't serve you. They just wouldn't wait on you. You sat there until you got tired and left. I remember one restaurant in Ruidoso called Brown's Café. We could go in there and eat. There were two slot machines in this little restaurant.

How is it today in Ruidoso? Well, it's changed a lot and I think the only reason why is because our economies are so tied together now. We have had to come together. Money has no color and has no boundary. I think that's our common bond right now. The economy. If it wasn't for that, I think we'd probably be back there.

I had a conversation with a white woman at the hotel in Ruidoso who told me that every one of the Apaches is rich from that casino, plus they receive a paycheck from the government every month, and they all get drunk and they don't work. Most of the time people are ignorant. They don't know. Sometimes, if they are worth enlightening, I do. But if they are just rednecks I tell them, "We are no different from any other people." We pay the same taxes. The only thing we don't pay is property tax. We don't own our property. It's in a trust fund. Everything else we pay for. So they shouldn't think we get off the hook. We pay everything else, even our gas. I have never seen a check come from the government to any of us.

And we are not getting rich off that casino.[6] You might think of other tribes across the nation who have gotten rich from their casinos. They are in a different situation than we are. Most tribes have a large population and are not paying per capita payments. With ours, we are lucky to pay maybe $1,500 a year. That's what we have been paying our people. That doesn't necessarily come from gaming, either. It comes from other sources, like our timber and other things that have brought in something. We have provided the $1,500 for years. Nothing is written or anything. It's not from the casino. As a matter of fact, there are rules and regulations against doing that. So the tribe has found other ways of paying it out to the people.

If you could say you did one thing as an adult, insofar as your work is concerned, what would it be? The major thing was working with road construction for quite a few years. I worked twenty-one years for the government on the reservation roads. Maybe seven years of my government service was done in Albuquerque. I was a regional road engineer. They hired me there, too, to run the regional roads for the BIA. I'm retired now.

Did you have time to get married? I was nineteen years old when I first got married. By the time I was twenty-six I had seven kids. I married a second time and have three children with that marriage. Ten in all. They're all doing well.

Something unfortunate really happened to me that changed my whole outlook on life. When I was twenty-six years old, I was a foreman on the roads for the BIA. I contracted arthritis and it just wiped me out. Acute rheumatoid arthritis. It crippled me. I couldn't walk. My dad had the same thing almost at the same age. I was out for a good two to three years with that. I couldn't work. I couldn't do anything. I was in pain all the time. I had to sleep sitting up. A good amount of that time I spent in the military hospital in San Antonio. I was there for two to three months. I also went to the William Beaumont hospital in El Paso. That's the last place I went. I called my dad and told him to come get me, that they weren't doing anything for me. They hooked me up to morphine and left me there all day. The wounded from Vietnam were coming in. They thought I was part of them and just herded me around. I was about that age anyway. My dad finally got me. The doctors said I probably wouldn't walk anymore, that I'd probably go around crippled. So my dad and I started working with Indian medicine, traditional Indian medicine, and I kept working with it, working with it. I remember an old lady named Maude Plata. She was close to my dad and so she used to come and bathe me in this damn awful smelly stuff every morning. It smelled like creosote. My dad used to bring the leaf and then my dad used to take me to those hot baths over in T or C.[7] It relieved me somewhat. After that is when I had the Ford experience.

In what way did this change your life? It changed my outlook on life, on the way I see my Indian ways. We were born and raised Catholic. Christians. I always had trouble with that because they didn't credit the Indian ways. Especially after I went through all the experience with my illness. After that I really didn't want anything dealing with the church. I kind of muddled up my first marriage. Life's too short. I wanted to do different things.

Today, Ed? I try to practice traditional ways. I still have my druthers with the church. I really do. I'm not very strong in my beliefs about the church anymore. My sister[8] and I don't argue about it. Over the years you can't believe a lot of things anymore.

And once again, today, Ed. In the way of job experience with the tribe, what positions have you held with the tribe? Maybe I should go back a little bit to my experience working with the Pueblo tribes. It pretty much is the same type of politics. I was working with the Ford Foundation and they had a project that was called the Community Action Programs. The university had a technical assistance arm of that and they hired myself and this other guy—a Puebloan. We got to be good friends and he became the leader after a few years. His name was Delfin Lovato. We had so much fun working together. That's how I got kind of connected with the Pueblos, even though my mother was from San Juan Pueblo. I have a lot of relatives over there. But I was born and raised here and registered here.

Delfin and I said, "Why don't we tell the Pueblos to contract this program instead of through the university. There's a lot of money we could use." The university was providing the technical assistance to the Pueblo program during that time. He and I rewrote the damn thing and got the Pueblos to buy into it. So they made me the director of the Pueblo CAP program. We started a consortium of Mescalero, Southern Ute, Ute Mountain, and Jicarillas, and all the Pueblos. As the director I got to do a lot of community work and gained experience. 1975. I worked for them. Delfin Lovato ran and became the vice chairman for the All Indian Pueblo Council. They impeached the chairman during his term so he wound up taking the leadership. We became pretty powerful, let me put it that way. Mr. Lovato had a lot of vision and he was smart and educated. A young whippersnapper. He could compete with the best. He and Mr. Chino here had a lot of respect for each other.

Mr. Lovato took over the whole thing so we reorganized the whole Pueblo Council, you might say, so it actually grew into a huge organization that was very powerful. We were once minus $20,000 in the hole and I was begging for money, trying to get it. I was able to convince them to use our ICAP[9] program for a year. It was going to be phased out anyway. I was able to do many things, grants, getting money, and turned it into a real large organization. I was policy administrator for that program from when it started. I spent twenty-one years in the Pueblos. I had some good experience to bring back here. Mr. Chino told me to come back whenever I got experience. And I did.

He called me up and asked if I wanted to be superintendent here. So I came down to Mescalero and was acting superintendent for two months. The BIA. I think I had a special relationship with Mr. Chino. I had a lot of respect for him and him for me. He always tried to help me. He knew I had the interest of the people at heart and he told me that. My cousin Freddie Peso was the same way. At that particular time Fred was the vice president and Wendell Chino was the president. I was acting superintendent. It happened to me twice. In the late 1990s also. I don't know entirely what happened. Mr. Chino at the time was totally supportive of myself and Mr. Peso.

You were recently a member of the executive branch of tribal government. The executive branch consists of the president, the vice president, the secretary and the treasurer. They are the executive committee. Well, during Mr. Chino's time, he invested most of the power in the executive branch. He was a strong leader, had a strong personality. He controlled it all. But he always had the council backing him so he never got in trouble there. He really, though, invested his power in the executive branch, which gave him a lot of power personally, also. He passed a lot of things that didn't go to the council. That's how it was.

Your roles in the executive branch? This is the second time you have come back to the tribe. I was the transportation director for the tribe for five years. Prior to that, when I first came down, the then-president, Sara Misquez, had called me up and hired me as the housing director. I worked there for about two years, when I first came back to the tribe in 2000.

My most recent position was as tribal administrator. There has never been a job description that has been made up for that. Mr. Chino was in power for forty-five years and he had, all those years, maybe two administrators. Dick Wardlaw was his first administrator. He vested a lot of power in him. It should reflect the management style of the president and the administrator should serve at his pleasure. But over the years the tribe has grown so much. I was frustrated with the current position. I told the president that I wasn't running anything because the job was too large. It should be reduced. It would be like a CEO. The administrator kind of functions as the chief executive officer of the company, which is the tribal organization. He oversees everything.

Another speaker complained that when an educated and experienced individual comes back to the tribe, there appears to be resentment and jealousy against him. Often the tribe chooses not to use his experience. Do you feel that pertains to you? Yes, I would agree with that because I have seen it myself among other tribal members who are educated and come home and there's no place for them to work. The tribe doesn't offer them wages anywhere close to what they offer someone else they brought in from the outside.

Why? I don't know if there's some jealousy involved. Quite frankly, over the years, and especially now, there's so much politics in the Tribal Council that there's a lot of relatives involved. Some of them don't like so and so, don't like that educated and experienced person. So they don't get a job whether they have education or not. That makes it hard. I have a hard time dealing with that. I see so many of our people like that. One of them is my brother Joe.[10] He's an attorney, one of the best Indian attorneys in the country, especially about the topic of water. He submitted a proposal to the tribe. They wouldn't hire him.

On the one hand you are saying they give jobs to each other and on the other hand they won't let some in. That's right in some cases, yes. Not all the time. My brother is educated and they won't let him back in. I don't know if it's because of education, family. It's hard for me to put my finger on it. It's not the people. That's what bothers me. Most of the people feel differently. They want their people to come back home. But it's the leadership for whatever their reasons are, whether it's political, family, or they think their relative is going to get into a position over you, stuff like that.

Has the tribe used your education and skills to your satisfaction? Not to the extent that they could have. I have had plenty of experience with just lobbying alone. The president and I went on a trip to Washington three or four months ago and the council got upset because they didn't know in advance. The president wasn't feeling well and didn't want to deal with all the council members, so he took me, knowing my background in lobbying. I lobbied for the Pueblos for years and was very successful in bringing money home for our tribes. He was impressed by me on that trip; that I knew about the system and how it operates and what to say. We went to Washington to do some lobbying, one for the fire program, one for housing, and a couple of other programs on the list. We went to all our congressional delegations and visited with each one and had good briefing points to talk from as a lobbyist. We were able to get in there and visit, including with Senator Pete Dominici.[11] We were lucky. Almost all of them gave us the time.

How did it happen that you are no longer a tribal administrator? I never was told officially that they didn't want me as a tribal administrator anymore. The president notified me but there was no reason given. He mentioned that someone said I hadn't performed. That was the "official word." I think a lot of it was a carryover from some road business that we got into a big hassle over. A contractor had a rock crusher on the reservation and they [the Tribal Council] claimed he was a thief. I told them he was not a thief. So they claimed I was in bed with him and getting kickbacks and all that.

Speaking of tribal politics, does it make sense to you to have a two-year term for elected officials? Well, at one time it did because the terms are staggered. The whole idea was to keep experienced council members on while new members were coming on. But now, it's lost. They're just all mixed up now. I don't think that holds any water anymore. I think we should go to a four-year term for the president and all the council members. If they want to keep staggered terms, they can do that with four year terms as well. My other opinion is that our tribe is large enough to have full-time council members, meaning now that people will really scrutinize them because they will be on salary. We want people who are competent in there who can do the business for us. A lot of the larger tribes have had to go to that. We need people who understand how complicated our tribe is and they can't be there part-time. It's just impossible.

With your vast experience and knowledge, working in so many capacities with Indians, do you see anything here on the reservation that frightens you? I guess there are several things that I see, some of it connects and some of it doesn't. I see a very poor future out there because we really haven't helped our young people. We have so many young people who are dysfunctional. Over the years it's so deep now, I feel, that it probably affects almost half of our tribal population.

Can you identify the origin of that dysfunction? I think the origin of that dysfunction came from alcoholism not being addressed properly with intervention. It has been allowed to continue. There was no intervention and there still is no intervention at all. From what I can see, what happened to us is that one dysfunctional child reached adulthood and another one was in the same boat. Two dysfunctional children wound up getting together, whether they married or lived together, and they wound up having children as well. I think a good majority of our social problems stem from part of that dysfunction.

How far back in history can you take it? Probably I can take it back to when I was a teenager in the mid-1950s. That's when it more or less came to my attention. Now that I look back I remember seeing something like that during that time. We were a small reservation at the time. Let's say there were no more than 2,000 population. Most everybody kind of knew each other. But I could see something happening there from the alcohol. People were drinking and their kids . . . you could tell there was something not right with them either. Because of their family not caring for them they were allowed to run free and helter-skelter. *So you see alcoholism as generational.* Oh, yes.

The other thing I see is the lack of understanding of our own traditional ways and culture. Too many of our young people really don't understand it or take it seriously. That's what I see has dwindled, along with the language as well.

The third thing I see is what's around us. We are losing our natural resources. They are not what they are used to be because people don't care anymore. There's not the interest. Yes, they get out in the mountains but for the wrong reasons. To destroy property. To kill animals. They are not out there because it's beautiful and they want to maintain it. They don't understand the forest anymore. When I talk to people about the forest they look at me like I'm nuts.

What causes that disrespect? I think it comes from those dysfunctional families. There's no respect for the elders, there's no respect for each other anymore. A lot of disrespect. You hear kids talking today, and we never heard them talking like that. To me it's not our tribe's fault; it's the greater society. When you watch TV, listen to that, and you look at our society here. Hey, we are not secluded over here in Mescalero. Everybody's got a damn TV and they watch every channel that everybody else watches in the city. To me, part of our problem is that communication is so fast that we don't even know all the stuff our children are exposed to.

Are these the modern weapons of the dominant society? Oh, yes. You're darn right. I've been involved and worked outside. For a time I had my own business as well. I was in the bonding business, but not to get them out of jail—I'd probably be pretty good at it—but I bonded construction. I got to work in the outside world. You scratch each other's backs and everything is done by helping each other. That's how the outside world operates. They pay you sometimes—the finder's fees. On the rez here there's a kickback and you're no good if you receive any kind of fee like that.

We understand that one of the problems affecting some native tribes is a conflict between the way they want to be and the way the outside world requires them to be. If you agree, can you talk about that? Yes, I think one simple thing was told to me one time by Mr. Lovato. He said, "Eddie, you have to remember when you are working with our tribes you are working with a nonprofit mind." Think about that. That means we were held by the federal government for years. Almost everything we received came from however the government wanted to give it to us. There was no such thing in our world as profit, as making money. I'm talking about the tribe as a whole. If you think about it, all tribes had a nonprofit mind. You talk to them about all these other things and they look at you like, what? To some extent it exists today.

Are you inferring that the tribe is going to have to become like the dominant society in order to be successful? No, I don't think you have to. I think you have to understand that we have to start thinking that, but in our own way. One of the things that we talk about all the time is our sovereignty. To me, sovereignty is only as much as you exercise yourself. It's a word. Unless you exercise that sovereignty, it doesn't mean anything.

Is sovereignty synonymous with self-determination? No. Self-determination to me is a whole different thing. It's a government thing that was created to make us self-sufficient with our money. I think what's happened is that gaming is really turning us around in terms of our thoughts on money, our thoughts on profit. One of the things I remember—I go back to Mr. Lovato's thoughts—is what he said. "We've got almost everything except one thing, Eddie, and that's economic. We've done everything we can in our power, created a political entity that's strong, because we have proved that we can deliver votes, deliver a candidate. But we still don't have serious finances." As soon as gaming hit we started getting serious. One of the things he always told me was, "The only difference between us and the white man right now is that they can afford to buy influence and we can't." If you think about it, it's true. Influence anywhere, whether it's Washington or the county level, local level, any level. People buy their influence. That's the way it is in the United States. You can buy that influence. We've made serious money now. We can start doing that. Contribute $100,000 to Richardson's campaign.[12]

But if your leadership doesn't understand that . . . That's true. You can buy all the influence you want but if it's not going to mean anything . . . *If you are here in Mescalero and the tribe has the money to influence the state or federal level, how do you learn to be like the white man?* You can buy it. You can buy good lobbyists that will be out there for your interests. You pay him good money and he will deliver for you. You might have to think like him. Right now I feel that our tribe is so enclosed. They don't travel around and they don't really deal with other business people in the sense that they should. Or even in the outlying communities. We have no relationship with Ruidoso. I mean a good relationship. That's what I'm talking about. Like with the mayor. Why can't we have a regular dialogue with the mayor of Ruidoso? And some of his councilmen. Only in a crisis we come together. That's one thing I notice that we don't do here. We can't see past our nose. Our leadership has no vision. Let me put it that way. That's what I have seen. "Vision" meaning where is our tribe going to be in ten years? Twenty years? There's no thought of that. Everything is just right here, right now in front of us. That's what frustrated me so much. There are so many things that we can do with some of the other resources we have that we are not using.

We should take some money and set up a development fund for our people to help them get into business. Or even build a strip mall at Mescalero. You need traffic in order to do business. We could build. Do like the outside world does. Build a building, rent it to them [tribal members], and then they don't have the expense of advertising. Pay for it if you want a small business. We have people who are beauticians; we have people who are artists that could be displaying their wares if we had a strip mall. If we don't do that ourselves, then it's a white man's world. Let's face it. How can a person be successful in business unless he has traffic? I'm using common sense. Why can't we do it? It doesn't have to be a white man's thing. You create traffic, people come in, they're going to buy from you. If we had a big supermarket there, we could set everybody's price around here. They wouldn't have to pay any taxes. They could get all their food from us here. There are so many things that we could do.

Please discuss some of the problems as you see them on the reservation today. We have been told that meth has moved onto the reservation. Do you see that as a problem exclusively among the young people? It extends across the ages and I think it extends a lot to the dysfunctional families that I talk about. I can almost pinpoint where most of them live. They don't vote, most of them don't work, and there's a bunch of them, maybe close to two thousand, in that predicament. They don't contribute to the tribe. That's half of our population. They just happen to live in certain housing areas. It's pretty evident. You can almost see it.

You can't close your borders to keep the drugs out. It's not a matter of closing our borders. It's law enforcement. Our law enforcement is poor here. I blame quite a bit of it on the tribe. The BIA has so much money that they allocate and that's it. There are never enough officers to take care of what we need. A lot of other tribes use their gaming money; for example, Isleta Pueblo. They have about the same population as we do, but less miles to cover. Yet, their complement of officers is about the same as ours. They used their gaming money to double their police force. That's what we haven't done here. We could do the same thing. We could have been doing the same thing but we entered into this bad arrangement that we now have with the Inn [of the Mountain Gods]. The debt.

To me, our social problems lead to a lot of the other problems. Why do we have truancy? Because of the dysfunctional families that don't make their kids go to school. All that goes on here. Our tribe has been real slow in keeping up with that. Now we have a truancy ordinance but look how long it took to get the damn ordinance. Now, what I'm concerned about is enforcement of that ordinance.

Speakers have said that health care on the reservation is one of the major problems. Sometimes we are part of our own problem. We have always had a hospital here and maybe it's not as good as we'd like it to be, but compared to a lot of reservations outside . . . They don't have hospitals anymore. They've got clinics, whether they are good or bad. To me, I would be far better serviced if we had a real good clinic. We'd go ahead and run it the way we want. But there's all kinds of ways to run it—third party billing—and other things that we could draw on. It wouldn't be exclusively for us, but how can we do it?

There's no way we can maintain a hospital for ourselves anymore. The health care we get off the reservation is poor right now. In Ruidoso it's really bad. They are not very good to our people. They treat our people badly there. Alamogordo is really good. We see the difference between those two. Hopefully we can use the Alamogordo hospital more.

What is the problem with the hospital here on the reservation? Number one, we shouldn't be a hospital. There's no use for a hospital for us. We can never fill our beds and then we wind up closed at night. We have to hire a full-time person then. We can get rid of all that. We can have a clinic like—I don't know if you have ever seen these Lovelace Urgent Care Centers. Then you have the expertise in that whole unit. When somebody comes in they can be referred to that specialist right away and then they are taken care of. Most of our people are referred to outside doctors anyway. So we have to lobby for more money for contract medical care. If we can improve our own capacity here, it would be a good clinic. Then we can really take care of our people. I would not have beds in that clinic. It would be like an emergency room. If the patient needs a referral he would go outside, hopefully to Alamogordo. We would make a deal with Alamogordo. Or, why couldn't we hire an outfit like Lovelace to come down and run our clinic for us? We could. Let them set up the clinic the way a clinic should be set up. It all comes back to money. So there's an even greater need to get money from the outside to continue.

There is a trust responsibility from the government to us, whether we be treaty, or however we were set up. The government is not living up to any of our needs. The government has pretty much abrogated all their trust responsibility to the tribe. What kind of health services are we getting? Not what we should. That's a breach of trust responsibility. Ours is based on treaty. We Mescaleros were one of the last tribes given a treaty.

How could that be enforced? How could you make the government live up to its treaty? The only way I can see us doing it is to file a lawsuit against them. We have done it here at Mescalero before. Mr. Chino filed a lawsuit, a breach of trust responsibility in mismanaging our forests. Twice. They paid us off in payments. The first time they gave us a million dollars. The second time it was 6 million.

Did they also fix the problem? No, they never fix anything. They throw money at it. That's always the way the government takes care of things. "Here's the compensation for us mismanaging it." It all comes down to money. Our land claims were compensated at whatever the price was back in those days. Twenty-five cents an acre, ten cents an acre. A penny an acre. Whatever it was. That's basically what they do. It's a breach of trust responsibility to the Mescalero Apache Tribe by the treaty. Our treaty was made from the 1873 executive order that set aside land for the Mescalero Apaches. The treaty also guarantees health care. It all states it in there. I have seen a copy of the treaty and then there's also the executive order that I have seen. The treaty created the trust responsibility between the government and the tribe.

If you could, what problem would you address first and how would you mend it? First, I think we need to fix our social problems, or at least attack them. I'm not saying you have to fix one here and one there. You can attack a lot of things at the same time. We can work on our economic future as well as working on our social problems. As far as I'm concerned, if we don't resolve those social problems, we don't have any future anyway. Who is going to run our tribe? Who is going to be here to want it? What if the government comes and says, "OK, we don't want to deal with you guys anymore. Here's your land." Just like they did during the allotment days. That's the part that scares me. We are not organized. I think we have to be organized like a city, like a state in order to protect our interests.

Could the council sell off, say, a hundred acres? It could happen. That's what scares me. To me, the only way to run this place is to go back to how the white man does, in the sense of a corporation, a corporate structure to protect ourselves. We can't count on the federal government to protect us. Who protects you on the outside? You have to have all sorts of protections to protect your interests. And if we don't do that, they will wipe us out in time. I think we need to establish a strong—I don't want to call it a government because sometimes you get hung up on government. To me, I see us more setting up as a large corporate structure. For profit. Instead of nonprofit. We have to. The government is not giving us the money they promised us. They're not taking care of us. The only way we are going to take care of ourselves is to make money. That's the name of this world. If that means we have to be like the white man, well, then so be it.

To me there's a difference between operating and functioning in the white society and thinking like a white man in terms of greed, in terms of their philosophy. We can't live without a TV, without modern conveniences. So if they say we are living like a white man, yes, we are. There's no doubt about it. Your clothes, everything you have. If you don't want to live like a white man, go out and live in the field. But, we have to maintain our traditions.

Ed, what is the future of the tribe? I'm kind of worried about the future of the tribe, because of our diminished forests; our natural resources aren't there. There's no reason why we can't have it. There's no reason why our timber shouldn't be productive. Poor management, on both the tribe's side and the BIA. Cattle herd, too. Poor management. We have no water in the mountains anymore, so where are the cattle going to graze? The cattle used to keep the forests clean so we didn't have the fires that we do. We didn't have to do the thinning because we had plenty of our cattle in our forests. They clean better than the deer and elk do. To me, if we don't improve that, our future is going to be fairly dim here at Mescalero.

What I see happening is that a lot of our people are going to move off the reservation for a livelihood. If we keep totally dependent on the Inn for gaming, I don't think it's going to last us forever. As soon as they open gaming to everybody else in the State of New Mexico, we will lose our edge. And the white man will build a bigger casino right in the middle of Albuquerque that will take everybody's business. It's coming, I think. It's going to happen. We put all our eggs in that casino at the Inn, that's not good. We have other energies that we need to look at on our reservation. Like I said, I don't know if we can ever salvage our timber but it's such a renewable entity, why not? I don't know why we can't save our forests.

What is your vision for the tribe? I would like to see our tribe as being one of the top in managing our resources. I would like to see that being one of our top priorities. I can see it happening. It's going to take money, number one, and a lot of money to get back in sync with our timber operations. I would like to see us get back in sync with our water. I think we can start improving. The ski run[13] is still a valuable resource to us and it can make us money. I have seen it make more money than even the casino. One season it made upwards of more than 16 million bucks in a three months' period, but it depends on the weather. It totally depends on the weather.

Will the tribe survive? I think we will survive. Maybe not to the potential I see unless we fix some things. For example, our education system is broken and without educated Apache people, our future is not very good. *But what about the backlash against them that you discussed?* This is where our tribe has to look at the young people coming back educated. They need to be elected into our council so our thinking can continue that way, rather than the old school that is still there. "Hey, I did it the hard way. You don't need a damn scholarship to go to school. I did it the hard way." Well, that's old time thinking.

Yes, I see us surviving. I think our religious beliefs are still strong enough to carry us through some rough times. Our leadership, quite frankly, over the years has not been very good at all. Mr. Chino was a powerful leader. He was good for our tribe. I think he lost it when he got the white man's disease of greed. He got greedy. Money. Not for the tribe, but personally.

A lot of young people today are dysfunctional. You can't have leadership or tribal survival if you depend on a bunch of druggies or alcoholics. There's where our tribe is going to have to intervene with that group of people. We are going to have to treat them differently. I don't care how you look at it. They are different. All the rest of the educated people, we are going to have to groom them to become our leaders. We are not going to have as big a trust as we should have because of these dysfunctional people. We have quite a few young people who are educated that we can rely on. They are starting to come back. We have a few on the council now. The point is they are appointed, not elected. See what I'm saying? They were not elected because they were too young, have no experience, but how else are our people going to get experience unless we involve them?

At least one of the horseholders we interviewed is terribly worried about the government taking this land and turning it into something else. Do you understand that? There's a lot of rumors plus a lot of ignorance on the part of our young people. That's where I fault the tribe. We need to have contemporary education for our people. I talked to Carleton about that. Information is really important. Even a simple letter from the president would help. He believes in information but he can't get himself into that mode where he can write to the people and explain things to them.

What is his reluctance? I don't know if it's reluctance, but sometimes I think it is just him not knowing how to do it and not knowing how to ask. He's a Ph.D. but that doesn't mean that you can deliver something to the people. We have tried to set up quarterly meetings for tribal members. The way they started was good, saying, "Here's what's going on with the tribe in different areas." That's what we have to continue to do. But in addition to that, I think—a lot of things are simple, but to the people they are not. Informational things, like where to get help, are just not there. Why it's important to vote. Apathy. Part of the cause of apathy is because a lot of the things we just don't provide to our people that gives them a well-rounded community. Things like activities for our people. We don't have a lot of activities, if you think about it. We need to look at more activities.

It seems like they feel they don't have an ownership in the tribe. That's right. I would say the same thing. Maybe it's because of the way our operation has been run for years. It hasn't changed. *And then, there's a small group of people who are involved and who are interested and they do carry the burden but then the other people get mad at them.* Of course. They are jealous. "You're getting more than me." There's always that little jealously that is created. It goes on and on. By family groups.

Now you have the outside influences of drugs and alcohol, so it seems like layer upon layer. That's true. Oh, yes. It's deep. That's what I am telling you.

Our problems are deep. We are not going to get rid of them overnight, either. No magic wand is going to cure everything. But I think one of the problems is that there is no intervention into it at all. We just keep putting a Band-Aid on the damn thing all the time. We are not curing it, that's for sure.

Are any young people becoming interested in leadership roles? Yes, I think there are. There are a lot of them that I think will do that. That's why I think I still see some hope for our tribe down the road. There's enough people who can take over. Retain the language. Retain the ceremonies. I think they may be easier to keep than a lot of other things. This is a low period in our history right now. Economically as well as spiritually to some extent. I have seen it lower.

Ed, is there anything we haven't asked that we should have? There probably is.

—September 25, 2008

TESTIMONY OF CLAUDINE SAENZ

I'm Claudine Saenz, a Warm Springs Apache. I am a direct descendant of Chief Victorio, Chief Mangas Coloradas, and of Martine, the scout who found Geronimo in the Torres Mountains of Mexico. My mother was Evelyn Martine Gaines, one of the last surviving prisoners of war. She died only a short while ago. I am a registered nurse by profession.

I was raised here at Mescalero until it came time for me to leave the reservation so I could go to school. I went to Arizona where I attended high school. Upon completing my stint in the military [Claudine was a marine], I returned to Arizona for college. I moved my children to Arizona. They could not communicate with the neighborhood kids, so they picked up the English and forgot the Apache. So that's what happened to my children. Although I spoke to them in Apache in the home they still responded in English. Families were trying to teach their children the English language and Apache wasn't spoken in the homes. The rationale was so children won't be struggling with the English language once they entered school. That's where it got lost. We were refrained from speaking our native language in the schools. We were reprimanded, sometimes swatted with a ruler.

Today I don't hear anyone speaking the native language in the community or in the schools. I substitute over there every once in a while and all the children speak English. Even if the old language were taught in the schools probably the children would still speak English because the teachers who are trying to teach our children the Apache language are not prepared themselves to teach the language. They are Apache; they are the ones who are trying to get it back, so to speak. They might speak a word, a phrase here and there but they could not carry on a conversation with me in the native language. That's exactly what's happening. They are the ones who are teaching our children. They would probably be my children's age, in the forties, and they are Apache people. The director of that school program speaks the language but doesn't practice it in everyday conversation.

The government had a huge impact on our lives by refraining the Apache students from using their language while in class and out on the playground or in the lunch line. This was probably in the '50s. That's when I entered kindergarten and I didn't speak a word of English. My first language was the Apache language when I started school. We had a teacher who would reprimand all the students speaking the Apache language, but that's how we communicated. We all spoke the language. I think she really had a problem with us speaking the language because she thought we were talking about her. She was a white woman who had a Hispanic last name. I think the person closest to having a college degree at that time was Mr. Wendell Chino[1] when he came out of seminary. There were no reservation people with college degrees back when I started school. Then probably when I was in about the fifth or sixth grade Mildred Cleghorn[2] became my home economics teacher and her husband was my fifth- or sixth-grade teacher. Those were the first two native people I knew that went beyond what I thought was as far as education could go. The Cleghorns were Indians from Oklahoma.

We were reprimanded for speaking our language, swatted with a large stick she kept at her desk. We never stood in the corner or anything like that but were pretty much swatted. And there was no reprimand for the teacher who did this. This was a BIA school. We accepted our fate because that's all we knew. No one told us otherwise.

Now the children are learning the language in the classroom that you were forbidden to speak. Is that "fixing" the loss of language? That's fixing the loss of language to some extent, but I don't know how long it's going to take us to get back to where we started. Probably generations and at this point in time, maybe never. *Do you believe the language will be lost forever?* I'm hoping that it wouldn't happen, but if we don't get things turned around and get our children speaking the language, learning the language, living the language, then it certainly will be lost forever.

Let's say that you have all the funds, whatever you need to reverse it. What would you do? They're still trying to work on a solution. They have the funds, they are getting the resources together, they're using us elders as a teaching source to develop different things for the students and for the people, and we can do it as native speakers. But if the recipient is not willing to learn, or have an interest, and says "Why should I?" then it's lost. There are very few who are trying really hard to learn. The youngsters, the teenagers, are the ones that, in this point in time, are not interested. They are kind of rejecting the idea because they listen to all the crazy songs they hear on radio and TV. They are influenced by technology. It's here in my home. My granddaughter lives with me. The music and the songs in the language are still here with us. The problem is passing it on and having them accept it and continue it. I don't know if the desire is there or not.

So they would rather see themselves as mainstream Americans? Yes. They know they are different. By skin color they know they're different. They know they are different because of where they come from. Who their parents are. They know they're different because they come from a rich tradition. But, there's always this attitude—"Why do I need to learn that? Why should that be important?"

Do they feel they are second-class citizens? I don't think that's the issue because we live with that. We know that we are second-class citizens. We are an ethnic group and we understand that. It's just all these things that are out there that they are trying to grasp, so to speak, and they prefer that kind of music to Native American music. *Do you actually believe that the younger generation accepts the fact that they are second-class citizens and that they just have learned to live with that?* Yes. They know that. *Who put that in them?* Probably their family. Probably we as a tribe. The teachers at school, the BIA office that was created here to "contain the people." The U.S. government.

Do the young people still respect their elders, parents, and grandparents? The attitude has shifted. You talk to these youngsters, whether it's in a school assembly situation, whether it's just one or two that you are trying to talk to and let them know why their behavior isn't appropriate and why they should respect themselves, respect where you come from, why they shouldn't talk in this manner, and they just give you a blank look. So you know that's lost.

That didn't happen in your family. At what age did you know that you were special as an Apache? When did your mother teach you and tell you the stories? Probably very early in life, maybe prior to entering kindergarten. How much is taught at home, I don't know. Pretty much somewhere along the line they are told that they are Apaches, that they are a unique people. Maybe there's no elaboration on that to say that we were important, unique, came from a strong traditional background. We know all the songs, the stories of where we came from, where we're going. These days those types of things were probably never told to the young people.

If there's a real strong grandparent in the home then that reinforces the teaching, but in a lot of our younger families, the grandparents are absent. The reason for that is that they died young from alcoholism. So these young people are growing up without the grandparents to teach them anything. Maybe these young parents don't know who they are, where they come from, who their relatives are, who they're related to, how they're related.

Others have told us that another weapon, besides alcoholism, that the government uses against the Apaches is inadequate health care. Do you agree? I certainly do. I would say so because, for one thing, our clinics and our hospitals, not only here but in other places, are not getting proper appropriations for what's needed in the clinics or the hospitals. There's never enough money and when we need something done, when we need surgery done, they tell us that's an elective service, so we have to wait until funds become available and sometimes that never happens. They just put you on a waiting list and that can go on for years and years. Who knows? Maybe it's their way of thinking that they will just keep us on the waiting list until we eventually die off.

During your career as a registered nurse, were you on the reservation? Yes. I have had all my nursing years with the Indian Health Service here at Mescalero, and although there are native people working in administrative services in the hospital we still have the same problem with funding shortage.

One of the obligations of the U.S. government is to provide health care for the Indian people. But if there are not enough funds, what is the government doing about it? What they are doing now is trying to get all eligible people enrolled in Medicaid—a state program—and, of course, some elders are on Medicare, but for a young family that has no income, they try to encourage the young children to be enrolled in Medicaid programs. And even that has its own stipulations, limits. Exactly. In some ways it's good, I guess. The state provides immunizations for our native children, reimbursed by the federal government. Getting medicine is no problem. Let's say, for instance, that if you have to go outside for surgery or something else that needs to be done, you bring your prescriptions back. They cannot fill your prescriptions because it's not in the Indian Health Service formulary. "We don't carry it here." So they give you an option. They give you the generics, change your prescriptions, or you take the prescription out and buy it yourself. A lot of times when they change that prescription, it doesn't work for the patient. They will try to give you something close but quite often it doesn't work. Some of the generics don't work.

Say I've been sick all night with an acute gall bladder attack and I go to the hospital. What happens? They will take care of you on an urgent basis. They give you pain medication for the pain to subside and if you are lucky enough they might admit you and observe you overnight and then refer you out the next day. If it's so acute that you do go out to the next facility, you are evaluated again by an emergency room doctor who refers you to the surgeon. Based on that emergency room's doctor's recommendation it's up to the surgeon who comes that night or waits until the next day to do the surgery.

Do you mean that I can go to the hospital in Ruidoso from the hospital here at Mescalero and the government will pay for that? Yes. They don't get paid right away because most of the time IHS is operating in the red. About six years down the line the bill will get paid but then the hospital submits our names to the collection agency because this bill isn't paid sooner. Really. The doctors downtown started to refuse to see us for a while until this COBRA thing came in.[3] Now they can't refuse services but find ways to brush us off.

A lot of our doctors come here just to pay back their loans from medical school. Some of them are just fresh out of school. Some of them are medical students. And then there are some that are good doctors. And then there are others that really don't know what they are doing and after many years of nursing I would point out to them that they might be wrong or "Let's try this," and they do that and it works. But the quality of care is not excellent.

What is their attitude toward Apaches? Most of them think this is an interesting experience. We're not that remote and the facility is not a big trauma unit. We don't have all the current, up-to-date medicines to offer and get our patients on. Then they get discouraged because they can't treat like they want to treat patients. Some of them sign on for six years. Some of them sign for a couple of years. Right now we are in an era where we have doctors under contract to IHS. These contract doctors work for six months, twelve months. So to them it's just a meal ticket. Payback. They don't have a personal relationship with their patients.

I first started my nursing career in 1970 and we had a tremendous turnover then. At that time we were getting doctors right out of med school under the Commission Corps. That meant the doctors had to be assigned to a military post or to an Indian hospital. That's how we were getting our doctors. Their rotation was two years. That was good because they got to learn the patients; they got to learn the ways of the people, that kind of thing. I remember one doctor said, "You know what, Claudine? When a patient tells me 'I feel worse somehow,' I know something is going on with that patient." He can get the jump on that patient and, sure enough, he can help that patient. It started to change probably in the late 1980s, from the Commission Corps doctors that we were getting. They were no longer going into the military because they were not being drafted anymore. See, the doctors we were getting were assigned here instead of going to a military hospital. Some would sign up for overseas duty. So that all stopped back in the mid- or late '80s.

What was it replaced with? We got replaced with whoever wanted to come here. Some were working off their loans. Some were just at the end of the line, ready to retire. They just come here to wait it out. Presently we have had contract doctors for the last six years. It's kind of like a nursing agency program. They have doctors sign up and then they send them to us.

Is there any attempt by these contract doctors to get to know their patients as individuals? That is not the trend nowadays. Most of the doctors that we get are either Puerto Ricans, Chinese, Koreans, Filipinos, and I don't know why. A long time ago they had to be a U.S. citizen to be able to work for IHS. We had a doctor who came from the Philippines and he was here about three years because there was no U.S. doctor to fill the post.

If I could change it, I wouldn't even know where to begin. I was in the clinic not too long ago and the waiting time was terrible. When I finally got into an examining room there was a gentleman in the next room. I don't know what he came in for but pretty soon he was almost in a shouting match with the doctor. This particular doctor came from Puerto Rico or Cuba or somewhere. Anyway, the guy got upset because whatever he came in for, the doctor was just going to change the medication. He said, "Well, I've been here for this problem before and I'm still having the same problem. You haven't done anything for me." So there was a shouting match. And then the doctor said, "If you don't calm down, I'm going to call the police." Then the patient walked out. He didn't get any medication, didn't get anything prescribed. He was really upset.

Then the doctor came in to see me, asked me how I was and what was wrong or was I just there for a medication refill. And he said to me, "I like a patient like you who knows what they want." And then he turned around to the computer. I said, "I'm glad I told you what I want because you are spending more time with the computer than spending time with your patient." That's the way it is now. They pull up your chart on the computer. There he is, sitting with the computer. He said, "You're right. I spend about 75 percent of my time on the computer and maybe about the rest of the 25 percent with the patient." And then that's it.

What do you see as the future of medical care here on the reservation? It's not going to get any better. A lot of our patients are referred out to Ruidoso or Alamogordo and then the people that work in those facilities say, "What are you doing here again?" The people in the emergency rooms at the hospitals, I mean. After a while I guess it becomes a problem for them and then it comes out like that when they see so many of our people. A lot of what happens here on the reservation is trauma stuff and when it happens it is all under the influence of alcohol. So they take on that attitude.

Some of the nurses have the attitude, "Well, I really don't have to work." They're there to work but it's taking care of people. So, that's the sad part from my perspective. When I worked upstairs with patients, my patients would be getting bad, I'd tell the doctor, "You need to send this patient out." A lot of the doctors would want to keep the patient and try to do as much as they can. They would say to me, "When you tell me what's going on with this patient, I know when to come." They had respect for me and sometimes the doctors would call me into the examining room and ask what I thought, what was my assessment. And I'm not a doctor but I would tell them and say, "Try this treatment," or "Do this." *Was that as a result of your medical knowledge or through the spiritual intuition?* Both.

What is the future, Claudine? Right now they are talking about doing away with the hospital and they are trying to make it so the patients go to outside doctors, outside clinics, and utilize what's out there. To me, that's totally unfair because they are breaking their trust responsibilities. They are not living up to that, as the government. Of course, all the money is going to Iraq. And so all our programs are going down. When that happens, health care is going to be a big problem. It already is a big problem. My last years working for Indian Health Service were 2000–2004. In the private sector a patient is discharged home the day after surgery. A lot of Indian people are not ready to go home then. They may be home alone. They may have somebody there. Say this patient is a female and the person there might be a male. Her son, her grandson. She doesn't want to be cared for by her grandson. And so they are not ready to go home. And then they don't take care of themselves. They start with infections or something like that. And then they end up back in the hospital again. They could get dehydrated because there's no one there to make sure they get plenty of fluids, get something to eat. So that's the problem.

What is the main medical problem on the reservation today? Diabetes is a big major problem here. Heart disease comes in second now because of the obesity and high cholesterol levels these people have now because of the high fatty intakes. *Where does alcoholism fit in?* Probably after heart disease, whereas it used to be the reverse. Alcohol used to be on top. Alcohol still is a big major problem but we are not focusing on alcohol now as we used to be. We are now focused on diabetes because it's starting early. Our earliest diagnosis was an eleven year old. Obese. Commodities play a part but the accessibility to fast food like McDonald's is one of the problems related to obesity. We don't have a McDonald's on the reservation but it is easily accessible off the reservation. And then overeating. When we were growing up in our family home, my mother prepared enough food for us to have one serving. There was never any extra. So we were happy with what we got. But now kids go for seconds and thirds. I see it in two of my grandkids, not the ones I have here but the ones that my daughter has. The two that I have eat a lot but not as much as my daughter's two. I told them to cut down on what they were eating, that they didn't have to eat like it was their last meal. But they acquired that somewhere. Certainly not from me. *The genetic factor maybe?* No, the television. They see all this food and are told to go out and be happy because you are drinking a Pepsi or a Coke.

The forced dietary change among Apaches that began on the Spanish colonial frontier has lasted through the generations and has resulted in dietary disorders, correct? Yes, I strongly agree with that, although they tell us there's a genetic component to all that and maybe they're right. I don't know. A long time ago the people used to harvest berries, nuts, whatever was in season. They jerked their meat. They did fine. That's how they ate it. Of course with all that physical work they did, they burned off the calories. Now, you don't see that anymore. The people eat and kick back and relax and turn into couch potatoes and before you know it, they have diabetes. Native Americans are more apt to get diabetes. My question was always, "If we're prone to diabetes and we carry the gene for diabetes, how many years back did that happen, or does it go way back to the time they came across the Bering Strait?" My mother always said that her mother had tuberculosis and she died. She said, "My mother never had a cough. Nothing like that." So was it diabetes? Her sight became impaired and she had weight loss. These are the symptoms of diabetes.

But I know the potential for diabetes began to show somewhere. Same thing with cancer. My mother said that her grandmother became sick and she didn't know what was wrong with her. They were living out in the feast ground area and she said, "I knew something was wrong but I don't know what she died from." And it could very well be that she had cancer of the colon. My mother didn't know because at the time she was going to school in Phoenix and they weren't permitted to come home during the summer. And that's when she lost her grandmother. But she knew before that something was going on. She may have succumbed to cancer. The symptoms suggest that.

How would you fix all this? Or must you stand by and watch it happen? Good question. I don't think it's going to stop. I think diabetes will kill us all. Something is going to kill us all and it will probably be diabetes. And then there's a lot of heart attacks when a person is prone to diabetes. You see a lot of that. Sometime they don't have diabetes but because of other things they get heart attacks.

Do you see the tribe being totally lost? Some time in the future our identity will probably be lost. We do have a lot of intermarriages and from this comes a whole different attitude in the way of thinking. Things are going to be lost. You can teach the culture to the people. You can bring it to the forefront but if the people you are bringing it to are not receptive then it's a lost effort.

How do you convince your children's and your grandchildren's generations of the importance of remaining Apache? You can offer it but in our language we have a lot of moral values and when you tell your children and grandchildren the reason why you do things a certain way, in your mind as a native speaker, you know what you're talking about because that's what you have been taught. You try to teach it to your children and your grandchildren and they ask "But why?" And you try to explain it. You tell them, "For one thing, that's how I was taught. I was taught this way and that way and if you don't do it this way, this and this will happen." And then they ask, "But why?" And we don't know the answer to that "why." Yet we know in our minds as native speakers what we are talking about, what we feel.

When you were that age, would you have questioned your mother? No. Never. Because we put it in our shoe and tuck it away. *And it's different today because of outside influences?* Yes. Most definitely. When my children were growing up and they would sit in front of the TV, I'd try to get their attention, and you can't get it. They don't want to hear the stories if it interferes with their television program. I see my grandkids doing that. I'll be dishing out food and they'll be sitting over here watching TV. I ask, "What's wrong with eating at the table? That's what the table is for." And then they will come back over here and sit down. There's no communication.

When did television come to the reservation? I was already out of high school when we got our first TV. I graduated from high school in '69, so it was somewhere in that area. And it was electric. We didn't have running water, we didn't have a hot water heater, we had an outhouse, but we had a TV because we had electricity. We had a refrigerator. We had a black-and-white TV and the reception was bad. We had to use an outside antenna. You couldn't get a reception with rabbit ears. You had to use an antenna and you still got a lot of snowy pictures. But it was a luxury.

When I was growing up and we were at my grandmother's house and when it was time to eat we sat in a circle on the floor on oilcloth. There was a little table with two chairs for my grandparents. We were only served a small portion to make the food stretch so everyone was fed. We sat on the floor and ate. And we were taught to be quiet when were eating. And I would ask my mother, "How come we can't talk when we're eating?" because we didn't do it in our home either. And she said, "Because you can choke on your food if you talk with food in your mouth." And we never did question her anymore after that. That's the difference between non-Indian and Indian. The area of conversation for non-Indians is at the table. That's where everybody talks. But as for us, it's quiet time.

Does it seem to you that the white culture with all of its consumerism is overwhelming this latest generation of Chiricahua Apaches? They are being influenced by what's out there—TVs, boom boxes, Game Boys, everything that is nontraditional. That is correct in that respect.

Many historians believe it once was the goal of the United States government to exterminate the Chiricahua Apaches. Are they trying it again? I would say slow but sure. Ultimately that will happen. In generations to come. I would say we are probably at the beginning of it. I don't know what kind of attempts will be made to try to stop it but I think we will ultimately self-destruct with bad food choices.

Do the younger people feel that way? My own children, my grandchildren, they know that they are Apaches, some of them are of mixed tribes, but they do identify with the Indian and that's because of our strong points. Beliefs. And then I've got two of them who participate in powwow dances. So, they have a real strong interest, a strong desire for that and also their Native American Apache dances and the singing. But the other children who don't have outside influences like grandparents, parents who speak the native language—I think it's totally lost. They can identify themselves as being Native American Apache but that's the extent of it. It does not mean anything. It's just an identity.

Aren't those two grandchildren some hope for the future? Perhaps they will carry it to their grandchildren. I sure hope so. I have fourteen grandchildren. Hopefully it's still there to carry. I can't say how far down the road. You have full blood Apaches on this reservation. By that I mean a mixture of Lipans, Mescalero, and Chiricahuas. They can still be full bloods but know nothing about their identity—where they came from. Our history is being lost but I see hope for the future in the language being restored.

—December 4, 2007

TESTIMONY OF SISTER JUANITA LITTLE, OSF

I am Sister Juanita Little, a member of the Franciscan Sisters of Our Lady of Perpetual Help. I'm also a member of the Mescalero Apache Tribe. My mother was a member of a pueblo tribe, the San Juan Tewa, now called Ohkay Owingeh. I was raised here on the Mescalero Reservation with my father's family with all the traditions, opportunities, and heartaches and so forth that the whole tribe enjoyed and benefited from. Although he was not Mescalero Apache himself, he had a great love for the people here and he used all his energy, all his talent, everything to improve the life of the people. I think he instilled that in all of us, my brothers and myself, and that's why I entered the Franciscan Sisters.

I am going on fifty-six years as a Sister. I started right in high school at the age of fourteen when I went to St. Louis to what they call the Aspiranture before beginning religious formation as a Franciscan Sister. I was there one year and came back home. My parents really thought I was too young to make such a decision. So I went to St. Michael's boarding school in Arizona for one year with the Sisters of the Blessed Sacrament. At that time I really knew what I wanted to do. The Franciscan Sisters of Our Lady of Perpetual Help accepted me as a postulant even though I was still in high school. I finished my high school as a postulant and started my college education in St. Louis at Webster College. My formation took five years.

I didn't know how it was going to happen, but I knew that some way I was going to come back home and make a contribution. How that was to be, I had no idea. So, it has been revealed to me as time goes on. My father has made a great impression on us in that area.

My father was the son of Andy Little who was brought here at the age of six by a band of Apaches out of Chihuahua, Mexico. This reservation's Botela family has always claimed us as members of their family, so it seems that that family took care of my grandfather Andy. And so I would just say that I'm Spanish, Mexican, and Tewa by heritage but by cultural heritage I always identify myself as Mescalero Apache. Because by an act of Congress the Little family was adopted into the Mescalero Apache Tribe, we are all known as Mescalero Apache.

Did your grandfather ever know his true family? I am told that my grandfather, when in his twenties, returned to Mexico to look for his family and did find his family, but his mother and father had already passed away. He brought back with him a few cousins who were educated in a boarding school here at Mescalero and then went back to Mexico. Our family got to know a few of them. We were in touch with them but as of about fifteen years ago we lost total contact with them. My grandmother—my dad's mother—was Mexican. We don't know her origin, where exactly she came from. Some say that she may have come from Isleta Pueblo, either from El Paso or near Albuquerque, but we can't verify that.

My dad went to boarding school. I don't have a boarding school experience in my early years. I do in my high school years. But, my father was raised in a boarding school, they tell me, from the age of six, here at Mescalero, and then later in Albuquerque. He finished the twelfth grade in the Albuquerque Indian School. They told me that during that time he was not allowed to come home.

My aunt, Sarah Peso, is at the Care Center here on the Mescalero Apache Reservation. She'll be one hundred years old on January 20, 2008. It's just in recent times that she has been telling me about her experience as a child. She, too, was removed from the home and brought to the boarding school here at Mescalero and very seldom went back to her home. My Aunt Sarah said the Botela grandmothers took her home on breaks from boarding school. Although my Aunt Sara's biological mother did live up in the Nogal Canyon area on the reservation my aunt tells me that she went to boarding school—Sherman Institute in Riverside, California—and then later on transferred to the Albuquerque Indian School. So she never really knew her mother; she was not in contact with her mother.

Why did the government take an Indian child into boarding school? From what I have listened to, and have read, the purpose was to enculturate the Indian people into white society, so they were denied learning their language, were denied the family practices and beliefs such as the puberty rite, which really brings the families together. They were denied living within the family unit where they learned the language and they learned the practices, the beliefs, and the other cultural practices of the family.

That was denied to the children, even to be raised as brothers and sisters, as in the example that I gave you of my aunt.

Do you believe the white culture intentionally instilled its values into the child so that the child was then separated from, alienated from, and divorced from his heritage? That was the intent, but I don't think it can ever happen. From my own experience, and from what I saw with my parents, even when they take on some of those practices, there is something inside of them that just cannot deny who they are. And you kind of begin to live in both worlds. You have to be a strong person to do that in your own identity. And there are many who have not been able to survive because they don't know where they truly belong. They don't belong in either place.

Let me just give you an example from my personal experience. My mother was Tewa and she, too, had the boarding-school experience throughout her life, but it was a little different than my dad's because her parents worked at the Santa Fe Indian School. So, they were there with their family. They had that strong family experience, whereas my dad did not. I think early boarding schools had some very positive influences because they did give strong vocational work skills. I heard my parents speak very appreciatively about that. But I think in the later years it got lost, probably in the '60s and '70s, a time when there was a lot of negative influence in the boarding schools. From my own experience, my parents did not want us to go to any boarding school or government school. We lived on the reservation, but we went to school in Bent [a nearby village]. There was a two room public school and I got the best education ever in that little school. I left there when I was in the sixth grade. My father transferred to Fort Defiance, Arizona, and so that's where I experienced Navajo children who went to boarding school and we who were children of Indian Service employees went to school next door. We were separated. That's the only experience I had.

The boarding schools today are quite different. There's one in Santa Fe that might be worth a visit to see how they operate. Those children get to go home almost every weekend. They have very close contact with their Pueblo communities. They have to meet certain academic qualifications to be in boarding school. It's not like they are yanking them away from their families and keeping them for years and years without any contact with their families.

What do you think of the boarding-school experience in general and its repercussions? I formed my opinion by reflecting on what my parents and other members of the family shared with me and by what I'm seeing here in the community among the parents and grandparents who had the boarding-school experience. My parents and my aunt and uncles who went to boarding school really talked about it being a good experience, good learning experience and interaction with other tribes. That is why there are a lot of intermarriages. But, when it came time for us to go to boarding school my parents didn't want us to have that experience. So I questioned: if it was so good why can't we have that experience? And then that's where the other stories begin to come out.

One of them that really struck me was when my parents were both talking about how they were used as medical experiments, especially with eye treatments such as trachoma. They called us "guinea pigs." Early school medical records show that both parents had trachoma so they might have experienced experimental treatment at the boarding school. They also saw the harsh discipline inflicted on other children. I suspect my dad endured some of this but he wouldn't say anything, not to us, but told other of my cousins who said, "You know this happened to your dad?" I was stunned. I still feel it because it was part of his upbringing. Other than being discriminated against, he was quite a football player and set some track records in the state at that time. He was quite an athlete. But once in a while he told us of their experiences in traveling to different communities for football games and how they were discriminated against. They couldn't go into the restaurants. Many times they had to sleep in the bus because they weren't allowed to stay at hotels. That was in the early 1920s. Every once in a while my relatives would speak about those experiences but not directly to us. As I said, they didn't want us to know that. So there were some good influences and some that they didn't want to talk about.

That's what I see now in dysfunctional families on the reservation. What I'm thinking is that the parents and grandparents who I know went to boarding school for years at a time, not coming home, not having that contact with family, stayed off the reservation because when they came home they couldn't really find their place here. And I can say that it's taken me a long time to find my place here and I still know that I walk in two worlds, but I'm comfortable now.

Do you have a preference? Yes, I'd rather be in my world here. We as a religious group of native priests, religious sisters and brothers came together and we shared our experiences. It has taken a long time for us to feel comfortable really living in two worlds, especially those of us who belong to religious communities. Some religious communities actually forbade their Native American members to have any contact with their families and any Native American practices. In 1979 I made contact with some other Native American religious and heard their stories. I was horrified because I did not experience that in my community. I'm the only Native American in my religious community and I never experienced that kind of discrimination.

Please talk about dysfunction, boarding schools, and the situations on the reservation today. I don't think every problem can be traced to boarding schools, but I think it has a lot to do with the dysfunction that I see in families. How can they establish a family when they have never lived in a family situation? And so they are not sure how to parent their children or even take that responsibility. So, we have the next generation—many of the children were removed from these parents because they could not really parent their children responsibly. These parents who came back from boarding school and tried to find their place often resorted, I really believe, to alcohol to cope with these problems. They ended up with a lot of health problems and early death, suicides, broken marriages, not being able to keep those relationships consistent or committed, and so these children had to be removed from this family situation and placed in group homes or foster homes off the reservation, which reinforced the negative circumstances. So here we are in the next generation, saying, "We're having some problems with this family and what can we do to keep this family together rather than break them up." And in some instances you don't have a choice but to remove those children. Where do you take them? Other members in the community don't want to get involved with them because it means family feuds or financial burden. So where can we take these children? Where do we put them? Again, off the reservation. So even though we are trying hard to keep our children here within their families and living within their traditions, sometimes removing them cannot be helped. The Indian Child Welfare Act of 1978 was designed to prevent the children from being denied their cultural heritage, but sometimes it must be done. My brother, Joe, had a lot to do with that act as an attorney. There again is my dad's influence—you need to do whatever you can to improve living conditions of our people.

The white society focuses on the individual, but the tribe's focus is communal. Is this one of the major identity problems the children faced when they left boarding school? That could also be contributing to dysfunction, as well as all the intermarriage into different tribes, and marriages to non-Indians as well. These marriages really cause an identity crisis because you're not sure where you belong. In the case of our family, my parents said, "We want you to be prepared to live in the dominant American culture." They tried to give us as much experience as possible in public school, not to separate us from them and the tribe, but to say, "You're not going to live here all your life."

And for families who did not have that vision, whose children went only to boarding school, you are saying again that that experience is one of the possible causes of the social maladies that we see on the reservation today? I strongly believe that. For some, they were able to overcome that and be strong because perhaps they had stronger family connections. Maybe somehow they were able to survive and be strengthened by that experience but for so many that was not true. And also to not have that bonding with their own because while you were in boarding school other siblings were being born, other things were going on in the family. I think there wasn't that bonding between family siblings.

Today our children are influenced by the outside world. It's right here in the school. And sometimes I get really frustrated by some of the people here who say they are traditional. I say, "Don't you see? Our children are living in a different world. They are having many different influences, experiences that are molding them." And if we think that only tradition is going to help them survive—it will help. I've gotten in trouble with some traditional people, not only here but elsewhere, saying, "Some of our traditional practices are really obsolete for us in today's society." I'm not saying they were bad, but they are not applicable to today. We need to establish new traditions that are going to be more life-giving for today.

For example, with regard to sexual abstinence, in our traditions we are not supposed to discuss that. During the puberty rites, the women explain this to the girls but otherwise don't talk about it publicly, or even privately. This is very, very private. You don't talk about it. But hey, the kids are bombarded with a very unhealthy view of their sexuality and anything that pertains to that from the television that they watch, the movies, everything around them. We've got to talk about it. And we've got to talk about it in a way that teaches the traditional values. We have to teach them with a different approach in the way that they understand it in today's world.

Look at the use of the tobacco. It's a drug and we have prevention programs here that inform the youth of the health risks of using commercial tobacco. Traditionally, tobacco is used in ceremony, not as an addiction. So we said, "OK, we'll look at this issue of tobacco." In fact, drug prevention programs are doing that now and are saying that even medicine men should use the real tobacco rather than the commercial because of all the substances and chemicals in it, especially if they are using it in healing ceremonies. In little things like that we need to become more aware that we just don't smoke every kind of tobacco. That's not the purpose of it. That's not a traditional kind of thing. We need to be more careful how we use that tradition.

Another problem you have said you are concerned about is truancy. We have a high rate of truancy in the community, not only from our school but from Ruidoso and Tularosa also. We have no way of tracking the students once they leave the school. So they may leave Ruidoso and say that they are going to enroll here in Mescalero but they never do and we have no way of knowing that. So where are they going to school? There's no tracking system. I wrote a letter more than a year ago to the Tribal Council and I got absolutely no response.[1] So, without that kind of authority, I really thought I couldn't move forward in developing, with the other liaisons from the other schools, a tracking system to monitor school attendance. The children are wandering out there even at elementary school level. That is detrimental for the future of our community, of our tribe.

In order to function successfully in today's world, whether it be here on the reservation or off, we have to have at least a basic education and job skills. *What is a basic education?* At least complete high school. I see too many dropouts. *What are the causes for dropouts?* I can only say what I'm seeing here at the school—a lot of behavioral problems exhibited by the children. Having lived in dysfunctional families develops real behavioral problems. Children see violence living in an atmosphere where there is alcoholism and other drug use. In such circumstances, parents just don't have control over their children and healthy skills. Lack of supervision. Parents are very interested in athletics. They'll be there for all the games and so forth. However there is very little interest in academic activities. In many instances parents are not responsible for getting their children up early enough to catch the buses. In elementary school we're seeing parents not getting up to get their little ones ready for school or neglecting health issues. These are examples that lead to truancy and eventually early drop-outs.

I just don't see enough educational encouragement. Many don't have the goal to achieve at least a high school education level. The message I try to get out to the community also is to encourage your children to get to school, attend school consistently, and try to do the best they can to achieve at least decent grades. Their school record and their school reputation is going to follow them through the rest of their lives. Even to get jobs or to go into the service—anywhere they go. I'm telling them that one of the most important things your kids have to learn in school—and I also tell the kids—is being respectful, especially to your teachers. I'm shocked sometimes at the disrespect, even to me here in the hallway. Some days I can be in the hallway with all the kids out there and you'd think I was invisible. I'll stand there and say, "When did I become invisible?" I'll say "Good morning," and try to greet each one, and some of them will barely greet me, some won't even acknowledge my presence. That's basic respect that we've learned in our tradition here, and anywhere you go. Acknowledging the dignity of another human being—I don't often see that acknowledgment and it disturbs me a lot because that tells me that they don't have a lot of self-worth of their own identity.

How do you fix that? That's what I'm trying to figure out. How do we fix it? How do I fix it? I fix it by presenting what you'll find in those letters, by reminding parents that they are the primary educators. Even when I was teaching in the classroom I always believed that the parents are the primary educators of their children. I, as a teacher, am going to work with them in partnership to educate their children, not only academically but in living their values. I want to know what family values they want to instill in their children. If they are good values, consistent with what I consider, I will do everything I can to help them establish that in their children for as long as I have them in my classroom. So, I'm trying to get over to the parents, "Yes, you are the primary educators of your children, you have the primary responsibility to see that your children get educated, not only academically but socially and spiritually. The school should be in partnership with you." What I'm finding is that many parents feel intimidated. They come when they are called because there is a problem. Of course anyone, myself included, would feel defensive and sometimes would feel intimidated by the principal. So that barrier becomes even thicker, stronger, that prevents positive interaction among school staff, the school community, and parents. They should be one community and that's what we are working at with this Mescalero Parent Encouragement Team Meeting.

I have to find a way to train the parents and I don't like the word "train"; more like giving them information about what the kids are learning here in school, what is available to them, and why it is important for them to get this education. What are the things keeping them from interrupting or delaying their education, which is usually the use of alcohol, drugs, and that usually involves the sexual activity that often results in teenage pregnancy. Teenage pregnancy doesn't only affect the girl; it affects the boy too. I see that around here. Usually their grades start going down, their relationships get really rocky, and so their attention is taken away from achieving in school and eventually they just drop out. She has to deal with the pregnancy, and he's being told that he needs to work or do something to support the child. It's hard for the boy to deal with this too. So they either drop out of school or their education is delayed.

We offer child care for unwed mothers. They can bring their children to school and take them to child care while they're in school. Child care is over in the elementary building. So there's no reason for them not to continue in school even when they have a child. But, even with that advantage I often see that they don't continue.

Do you see this frequently, or are you thinking of just one or two occasional instances? Last year we had eight pregnancies, a lot for this population of five hundred plus kids who come to this school. *Is that the influence of the white culture?* I think so. I have spoken to some of the traditional people, especially the women who sponsor the young girls in puberty rites. "Tell me," I said, "is there something in those rituals that encourages this kind of practice?" I'm not understanding these girls who have gone through the puberty rite. Shouldn't they have been counseled, advised? There has to be some other outside influence. Perhaps we are allowing the dominant society to have more influence than we want to admit.

Do these problems affect the future of the tribe? Do you see the survival of the tribe or its demise in future generations? I would say survival of the Mescalero Apache Tribe. I am optimistic in that sense. Survival because we have many out there that see the problems we are facing in the tribe and are willing and capable to confront the problems that threaten our survival. *Are you referring to young adults?* Yes, definitely. And I'm very glad to say it's the same people that I taught in catechism when they were little, and I'm working with them now and—oops—I'm calling them by their first name when I'm supposed to be very professional and call them Mr. or Mrs. It's so wonderful to work with them on this professional level. Having to relate to them on a more professional level, sometimes I forget that they are now capable adults. Each time we get a new administration, I notice that they are more and more educated. But there are so many attitudes we have to change about our social environment. A lot of time has been spent on developing the tribe's economic base with the hope of making employment available for everybody. But, I'm saying to them, "Because of all these other social problems we have, it's handicapping a lot of our young people to gain the skills to be able to be in higher positions in our enterprises."

Will you talk about the social problems? Alcohol and drugs, they go together, and early pregnancies are definitely an issue. Truancy and dropping out of school contribute to the high-risk behaviors of our young teenagers as well as our young adults. There is a lot of violent behavior. When I worked with the domestic violence issue, I became aware that many children are really living in very traumatic environments that are disabling. And that's what we're seeing with some of these behavior problems. They can't function in the family, they can't function in school, they can't function in ordinary situations. Should we send them away? Send them off to somewhere else?

Sister, in a school situation, children compete. Are competition and its benefits lacking? Yes, because that's how we operate. We don't encourage competition. There's nothing there to encourage competition. I'm saying to a certain extent competition is good. Of course we have examples all over in which competition has gone awry, but I think a certain amount is good. *But if you think community first and tribe first, you don't think competition.* That's right. That's why I was saying that there are some things we have to rethink. Certain attitudes were good for us at a certain period of our history but there are certain other attitudes and ways of doing things that we need to adapt. We are adaptable; otherwise, we wouldn't have survived this long.

I was talking to another tribal member and I said, "our programs are really hard because they emphasize kids having to set goals. Goals aren't one thing we do well." "No, we don't," she said. I asked, "Why is that?"

And she said, "Because we are still in the survival mode." Yes, we are still just surviving from day to day. We're not thinking of next year or ten years from now. I thought, "Now I can understand that." Since she said that I have become aware and I believe she really hit that on the head.

Survival mode vis-à-vis the U.S. government? Just to live from day to day. Includes the government, includes the churches, includes the schools, includes the social institutions. Includes everything. Just to live day by day.

Obviously, thirty years ago there weren't the same problems that exist today. When you were first back on the reservation, in 1978, did you see as many problems as you see today? That's a difficult one. One of the differences I have seen over the years since 1978 is that alcohol continues to be very prevalent, with the introduction of other drugs—marijuana, cocaine, and now we're dealing with meth. Previous to that, I was appalled that at our feast, at our dances, it seems that you could smell the alcohol coming off the singers, the dancers, while they are doing their rites. But I really have noticed a big change. You don't see that anymore. It happens, it's happening out there—on the outside of the circle. Alcohol is prohibited; it's not within that circle that's doing the ceremony. Before it was right there in your face.

Earlier, when I was at the church teaching catechism to the children, I had contact with the people who were probably not as much involved with drugs and alcohol because I was with people who weren't doing it. As I came back into the community and was going out to the people and visiting, then I became more aware of the impact that drugs and alcohol were having on family life. I didn't name it then because I didn't know how to name it until I was more focused on what the alcohol was doing. I started going to workshops that they were offering here in the community on what alcoholism meant, what addiction meant, and then I began to learn that I was being an enabler. The church was enabling.

How so? We were enabling because those who were coming to us inebriated and so forth, yes, we were giving them food, trying to help them out materially. You'd think that was fine. But they needed more than that. They needed somebody to listen. This is when I, even when they were inebriated and still talking at least coherently, listened to them. I would sit down and listen to their story. That's when they would tell me their pain, their sorrows, and then I began to realize, "Ah, this is what's at the bottom of this alcoholism." The priest and I would listen to them but I was thinking, "OK, I need to do more than this. I'm enabling them." I was angry at the church because I thought that we were doing nothing to help these people. But, I didn't know how. None of us knew how to help.

What are the good things the church has done? One of the priests and a brother who were here started an AA meeting and that was done right at the church. They held AA meetings for about two years and after they left it continued for a couple of more years. One was a recovering alcoholic and was able to relate to the men—mostly men—coming to the session right at the church. I was happy about that because I thought we were doing more than just listening at that point in trying to understand what was at the bottom of their use of alcohol and drugs. And understanding that a lot of the violence we were seeing was not the result of alcoholism but was exacerbated by that usage. There were other issues going on also. So that was one of the things the church did for some time.

In the meantime, residential alcohol treatment had been established. The church has supported this treatment center by actually working there. The Franciscan Brothers worked there. I worked there also for almost ten years as a caseworker and made presentations on spirituality, not trying to promote the Catholic faith, but just trying to get them to recognize their own spirituality and the value of their own spirituality no matter what tribe they may be from or what denomination they belonged to. So, wherever I am, I definitely feel that, even though I was not working directly out of the church, or sponsored by the church, I am still doing ministry for the church.

We also have a food program that all churches on the reservation are invited to support. It's available as an emergency food program to help people for two or three days until they can get assistance.

I guess I just see a lot of positive things. We are far from doing all that we need to do but I really have to say that we Franciscan Sisters really have given continuity to the Catholic religious education and formation. The church building restoration project has also made employment available.

Speaking of continuity, I want to ask if you think the ancestral language and culture will remain into the future. I hope so and I think it will because there is a big emphasis in school in instilling the ancestral language. It's taught in regular classes. Not just the language but the music and the art, history. Yes, I agree that language, beliefs, and cultural practices are taught more effectively at home in a family setting. However, a lot of families have lost that, too, again because of boarding school. They didn't learn it.

May I interpret your use of the words "boarding school," both literally and figuratively, as meaning the white influence that deliberately excluded tribal customs, tribal ceremonies, tribal language, everything. Ethnocide. Yes. And sometimes not deliberate. In my case, when I went to Catholic boarding school they did not deliberately seek to separate me from others but out of ignorance they didn't know. They didn't know anything about my customs, and I didn't share it with them because I was the only Native American. They would introduce me as Apache or Native American. Right away these people would assume, "How come you're a religious? This is a big thing." And I'm thinking, "Why is this such a big thing for me? If the other girls were not Native American it was OK and you could expect it from them. Why can't it be expected from me?" So I tended not to share anything from that part of myself. I was taking in all the white stuff because to survive there I had to do that. But not because they were being mean. There was such a lot of ignorance of native peoples and I wasn't old enough to try to explain all this or try to figure out what was going on. It wasn't until years later—when I was celebrating twenty-five years in the religious community—that I finally realized something was missing in my life terribly. After twenty-five years of being a Franciscan I should be celebrating and I should be whole but I was feeling this horrible emptiness. I'm feeling that I don't even know who I am. I'm feeling really drawn to go work with any native community. I had been away so long. And I thought, "What is going on here?" I really was going through an identity crisis, until I met up with other native religious of the same age and we had the same stories. We couldn't deny that part of ourselves. I had been denying a part of myself and I was at the process where I needed to integrate the whole. And I said, "What's missing here?"

I finally came back home in 1978 to teach in Alamogordo and live in Alamogordo where we have a school. And in the afternoon I came up to Mescalero. I had no idea what I was going to do. The Reverend Mother came and said, "OK, you've been up here two years." I thought, "Oh no, they're going to tell me no more of this. You haven't accomplished anything." At first I was cleaning the rectory and cutting weeds to make a safe and welcoming place for the Catholic community. I was going according to what Father Albert Braun, a beloved priest, had said, that if you are going to minister here you have to go out to the people. The next step was just to get out there among the people. And I did. I went knocking door to door. And when I knocked on the first door, I thought, "I'm bringing back the faith and all of that mentality about being this great missionary." I can still remember so well. It was so strange. There were sparks flying all around. This person answered the door, invited me in, and I identified myself. Of course, as soon as I said I was Bernard Little's daughter, there were open arms immediately because Dad was so well respected and loved in the community. The people hadn't been practicing Catholics but they knew the Catholic faith. They had the rosary hanging on the wall. And they knew their faith. I thought, "Oh, boy. I'm not bringing the faith here. It's already here. What am I doing?" So that was my first experience and the sparks were flying. The Holy Spirit was telling me, "I'm already here."

Are you the only Native American in your religious community? Yes. I've heard some others claim some tribal ancestry but I am the only member raised on an Indian reservation.

Referring back to a previous discussion, what will the future bring for the tribe? Or will there still be a tribe? I think we will still be a tribe, I really do, because the people are resilient. The government has treated us as children far too long, and we have to grow up and stand up for ourselves and make decisions about what is best for all of us. I think we are going in that direction. We may have a lot of problems, but that reflects other problems that are going on nationally. But I have seen more and more younger people recognizing the problems and stepping up to the plate to do something about it.

If the tribe survives, is it possible that the people will not necessarily be living on the reservation? Oh, yes, it's coming to that. That's the fear I have. Should that happen and we don't have deeds to our land . . . If it happens now, if the reservations are terminated in the next five or ten years, we are not prepared. We need to prepare for that by making sure we have deeds to our land. I want people to realize that in order to hold on to our land, we must make sure that we have legal ownership of the land.

Sister, you believe that the tribe will survive. Does that mean the language, the prayers, the ceremonies, the culture? I think it will. I definitely think it will. Like the church, we are a living, growing culture. Externals will change but the essentials, traditional beliefs, values, and perhaps even language will remain.

—December 5, 2007

Conversations

THE WARRIORS

TESTIMONY OF JOEY PADILLA

Dedicated to my wife Thora Padilla, my son East Padilla, and my daughter Aspen Padilla

I'm a half-breed, half Mescalero. My mom's from Mescalero, my dad's from California. Been living at Mescalero all my life. My family comes from a line of medicine people, sixteen generations back. Our original place of homesteading was in Rinconada.[1] That's where my great-grandfather and my great-grandmother came from. My great-grandfather came from Mexico. He was a Lipan Apache. My great-grandmother was a Mescalero Apache. So my family ranges from Rinconada. Probably in the 1950s we moved back to Mescalero and homesteaded there. That's where I've been all my life. Went to school in Mescalero and went to high school in Tularosa. That's where I graduated from. I went to college in Santa Fe for two years, got my associate's degree there and then went to art school in Minnesota to pursue my education at the Minneapolis College of Art and Design. It's sort of a private school, hard to get into.

Have you done anything with your art? Yes, I still work at it. I still sell it to different people. I do jewelry, I do sculpture, I do paintings.

Are you married? Do you have children? Yes, I'm married to Thora Padilla. She's from Mescalero also. She graduated from Teddy Roosevelt High School in Texas. She now runs the Environmental Protection at Mescalero. I have two kids, a daughter named Aspen Leaf Padilla. She also graduated from Tularosa High School and is going to college now. I have a fifteen-year-old boy who is going to Ruidoso High School right now and he's in the rodeo circuit. That's why I'm here at Cow Camp,[2] working for him, for his future, and for the future of the tribe. Today I'm working here at Cow Camp as a cook and an assistant to the manager. I do the monthly report writing, I do the bills, also, and cooking three times a day. I get up at five o'clock in the morning and have breakfast ready by six for the cowboys and hope they have a good day. I have a smile on my face, say "Good morning" to them every morning. That makes the day.

How have you been able to instill the desire to get an education in your children? The reason why is that most of my family never graduated from college. We all graduated from high school but most of us have never gone to college. I pursued college, and maybe somewhere down the line I'd like to get my master's degree. To further myself.

You are a medicine man. Do you practice it in Cow Camp? I set it up here. I'm putting up my tipi now and we are going to start practicing probably tonight. David, the manager here, is one of my students. I've been teaching him for about six years now. His boy is into the medicine too. My son and daughter are both into it. As soon as my daughter gets through with her college, my mom will be passing on her medicine to her and I'll be passing on mine to my son. He knows a lot. When I was fourteen, I had my first feast, and he was fourteen when he had his first feast. It just happened that way. It all falls in line. So there's a reason for everything. The "man upstairs" always watches over everybody.

How does the government interact with the people on the reservation today? To me, the government should get out and let us run it ourselves. They are killing us by taking control, like the BIA. We don't have to report to them anymore, but they still have a handle on our Justice Department and the police. They should turn it over to the tribe. The government was designed just to help us get things going, but now they're still here. We already have our enterprises going. We are making our own money. What do we need them for? Really. Like the forestry. Why can't it be tribal? Why does the government have a hand on that? Because it's the land. Forestry does things with the land. If we get rid of them, then we don't have those kinds of problems. It will be all tribal. The Environmental Protection was started by my wife. The government wanted to put a handle on that too. She said "No. Why can't I run it?" So she does. The courts too. The government has a handle on that also. Why can't we have our own Justice Department? Like the FBI coming in and taking control whenever they want to. It's not right. We have our own people who can do the work. We have our own investigators who are tribal people. That's why we go to school.

Our advantage over the white man is education. They gave it to us.

Just like the gambling. We have gambling because the white man showed us how to make money. So we used the white man's knowledge against him. Now they don't like it. So that's one way we make money.

One leader never led the Mescalero people. It was always five or six leaders. What's better, having one hand or five or six hands? So, if you get rid of one, you still have four or five following. That's the way the Mescalero people always ran it. *Is it still that way today, other than the Tribal Council?* Sometimes. Yes, I think it is. It's just like us in the medicine tipi. When we ask something, we all decide on it, not just one person. We ask all the medicine people how to handle a problem so we have all the opinions. When you have all the opinions, there's no fussing and moaning because you already agreed on this.

How would the Chiricahuas handle this? The Chiricahuas do their own thing. They prefer to do their thing by being one. But we are all one now. Everybody decided to be one. Not just one person decided for everybody. It's best to have other people's opinions and thoughts. That way you get further and further into what you are doing. In other words, your problems are solved. Your problems that you want answers to are solved also.

Are you saying that the medicine men all get together and have their input is a good thing? It's a better thing. Everybody has their differences. Just like you live differently even if you live together. You still live differently. You use different shampoos. But when it comes to a decision on groceries and stuff you still combine it. When you go shopping or pay bills, you both combine it.

What is the role of the president [of the tribe] today? To make the right decisions for the people. *With the input from the council?* It should be, it should be one for all and all for one, as the white man says. *You're quoting the white man?* Why not? *Can you imagine the U.S. Senate reaching a consensus with no leader?* Yes, I can see it. They would probably live a lot better. Maybe they could sleep at night.

How can you reach a consensus with everybody's input? Got to have one person do it. Have a good thought in mind to convince people. Prayer should always be first. A lot of people don't practice that any more. The Apache people always give a little bit of something first. That's just the way it is. The more you give, the more you receive down the line. It doesn't happen in big quantities. Little bits, little pieces. It's like getting us wild. You give us a little piece of something in us to get us wild. Then the whole thing gets wild after a few days. It's always bits and pieces. It's never the whole thing.

Going back to talking about the land, are you suggesting that all this would become private land for the Apache nation, and not a reservation? To me, if it ever changes, which it won't because we're not going to let it happen . . . that this become private land. This is everybody's land who lives here. It might not be called a reservation. It's like shell shock. Now you have all different kinds of names for shell shock. It's still shell shock. *If you got the federal government, the BIA, out of here, it wouldn't be a reservation.* Well, we should. Yes it would be. It would still be a reservation. It would be a Mescalero Apache Reservation then. It would be ours. We wouldn't have to answer to anybody. They should think about what sovereignty really means. Sovereignty is a big word. It's not a small word. It's a big issue. People do not know how to use it.

Tell me about sovereignty. To me sovereignty is being on your own. Always on your own. To make things work for the people, for whoever wants sovereignty. Sovereignty is freedom to the Indian people of the United States. It's a big thing for them. That way we don't depend on anybody. We depend on ourselves. And we should always depend on ourselves. Back in the 1800s we depended on ourselves anyway. Why not? That's how we survived. Sure we ate fats. But we were healthy then. We still can be. We just have to change some ways, start eating better and better.

Some Apaches are very afraid that the land will be taken away from them. Not while I exist. Have to kill me first. Nobody is going to take this place away. Someone told me that when you learn something the only person who can take it away from you is you. It's just like cancer, diabetes, diseases that are in your body. The only person who can take it away is you. If that doesn't happen, you are in trouble because then it will take over you. They always told me, too, that if you want something done, do it yourself, then you know it's done right. It's the same thing here at Mescalero. If we don't do it ourselves, it will be taken away. And that includes 460,000 acres that we own here. And 4,000 Indians that live here.

In what other areas is the government today trying to kill Apaches? The airplanes that fly over us. To me, every time these guys fly over us with their jets from Holloman Air Force base, the people start getting sick. Airplanes fly above us especially at night at about two hundred feet up in the air. *Two hundred feet above the ground?* Yes. I've seen pilots fly so low you can see their faces in the jet. They are spraying biological warfare on us. Testing. What do you think those vapors come out of the planes for? All of a sudden there's an epidemic of walking pneumonia. Why? All of a sudden you have an epidemic of cancer. Why? Never was here before. Then they started flying over and these things started happening. Our [the United States] mentality is like Afghanistan. You have to get rid of them [in this case, Apache] somehow. There's more than that happening here. During seventeen years of being a game warden, I used to see it all the time. First thing was getting sick. How come flu just happens like you snap your fingers? All of a sudden the kids are getting sick real fast. They are experimenting on us. They are killing us off too. If they experiment, they would have to do the spray, cause the flu, and then be able to do a census afterward to say that on March 1, we sprayed. That's why you have IHS [Indian Health Service]. IHS is run by the government. Doctors are run through this place like cattle. Every time we get a doctor, next month we have a new one. Now we're getting doctors from Mexico, Puerto Rico. Why? Guinea pigs, that's what we are.

Tell us more. The medicine they give me for diabetes is two years old. We should have different medicine here. If you go to a private doctor and show him the medicine, he will ask, "Where did you get that?" Some of these people are taking fifteen to twenty pills a day because it's prescribed for them. I have a cousin who takes all those pills for diabetes. He lines them up and it takes him a whole day. I told him to throw them in the trash and let me heal him. We're just guinea pigs here and we're beginning to realize it. All the reservations in the United States are by air bases. Look at it. They have air bases right next to them. *So you think this is widespread across the country, not just here?* It's everywhere.

When I was a kid, six or seven years old, I used to have really bad asthma and was always in the hospital [on the reservation]. So they took me to a [government] hospital in Albuquerque and came to find out that every day they were giving me steroids to get rid of my asthma. They have records on me. When me and my wife were trying to have kids, I was having a hard time because my sperm count was so low. It was because they had given me steroids every day for a whole year when I stayed up in Albuquerque. It affected my reproduction. *Do you think that was the deliberate intent?* I don't know what the intent was. Back in they '60s they experimented with steroids.

My mom worked in the IHS hospital for twenty years. We used to have a lot of birth defects here because they experimented on the women with birth control. Back in the '60s. Pretty soon you have kids who have a cleft palette, also have one ear, their eyes have dropped down.

Besides the airplanes, what's going on today? Water. Our water system. Sucking us dry by putting their straws into the ground and sucking it out. By underground wells. Submersible tanks. All around us, especially Three Rivers,[3] the most important place. Three Rivers has the purest water because it's filtered through lava rock. The government has two tankers come every day for water. In plain view.

It's just like the WIPP site.[4] You should see what they have at White Sands. It's uncovered now because the sand is moving away. Now all the nuclear waste is coming out of these barrels. They found a cat. They found nuclear waste barrels, nuclear waste suits again uncovered that were buried there in the '50s.

When they experimented with the atomic bomb, they didn't tell the Apache people about the atomic bomb. My grandmother said night became day real quick and the earth shook. She said we used to have exotic birds here and they all died out. Everything changed. We used to grow palm trees. I have pictures of my great-grandmother's house with palm trees around it in Rinconada. And now you can't even go there. They said even a thousand owls came through Mescalero to tell the people to leave [before the atom bomb was detonated] because there was a disease coming through. The ones that stayed died. The people that went to [areas like] Whitetail, Rinconada, Elk survived. They were warning the people that something was coming.

I work with a lot of grave sites here. Every grave site that we have uncovered shows that they were burned. They burned the people because of that disease. You can see it. We uncovered one that had a little boy on the bottom, a teenager, and then an adult on top. Everyone was burned because of that disease. *What disease?* From the bomb, or it could be from many things they were experimenting on us. Radiation. Just like my grandmother said. The exotic birds were from Mexico. There used to be a jungle around here they said. And when they blasted that atomic bomb everything died. What you're looking at right now are shrub trees that don't belong here. Shrub trees that take the groundwater out and dispose of it. That's what's left here as a consequence of that bomb. It changed a lot. Threw everything out of balance that we are trying to put back together but we're having a hard time.

Will you talk about the influence of the white society on the young people? Someone has to care. It's just that. Sure, TV, videos, drugs—white society, alcohol—white society, it's all white society. Even into the Mexican world. White society has affected them also. Taught them how to put gangs together, how to put drugs together, how to make drugs. The white society has done that. Same thing with alcohol. White society has done us damage and it continues. There's no end. It's control.

We have been told that meth has taken over. Probably. But control is not the big issue with all that kind of stuff. They need help and we don't want to give them help. *The youth?* Yes. They're bored. A lot of them are bored. A lot of these young people need something to do every day because their attention span is short. Just like when I was teaching high school. I wanted to see where the teenagers were this day and age. My day and age was different. I'm fifty years old. But what is happening now is that they have no sense of who they are. Identity is a big issue. *What do you mean? Cultural or personal identity?* They are running around with nothing. Trying to find something. They don't know who they are. *Do you mean they have no connection to the past?* That's right. Now they're making it in school so that you have to learn the Apache language before you graduate. A lot of them told me, "Where is it going to get me? When I fill out an application for work, is the Apache language going to get me that job?" Look at their side. Look at what these kids these days think. "I'm not going to use it everyday." Are my kids going to learn it everyday? Really. *Don't they need it for the songs and prayers?* Yes, but they don't care about that either anymore. It's only a handful that cares anymore. They depend on the handful of people. That's it. I wish there was a turnaround but they're right. It's not going to get them a job. The white society will tell them they have nothing. If you don't get an education, you don't have anything either at Mescalero. Most of these kids go into the armed forces. They go to the Marines because they are taken care of. They go to the Navy because they are taken care of. That's their future. That's how they get their college paid for these days. Because the people here at Mescalero have taken it away from us, our age.

Like I said, there's only a handful that care about our traditions, and it's always going to be like that. My aunt in California is ninety-something years old and she told me that we are wasting the language in the school. The language is everyday, from the time you wake up at home until the time you go to bed at home. That's where the language begins. Not at school. School is just a tool. You get thirty to forty-five minutes of language and then you're out of the classroom and you go to the next room where all they speak is English. What's it going to do for you if you were an Apache kid? Put yourself in their place. It's not going to be very good because you're only going to pick up a few words here and there to get you by.

Are you suggesting that the language not be taught in the school? It should be taught in the home. *But that's not happening.* That's right. It's never going to happen because our lifestyles are so different nowadays. Look at what we are wearing. If you are an Apache, where's your dress, your Apache belt, your moccasins? This is what society has done to us right here. Changes your clothes right away.

How do you reverse the trend toward becoming white people? You are saying that the influence of the white society is turning Apaches into imitations of white people. How do you fix it? Have a lot of prayers to the man upstairs to change a lot of people's minds. I call him the "man upstairs" because he's always higher than anybody. When I speak my language I use the right word, but when I give interviews like this I say the "man upstairs." I just pick up Christianity here and there.

Since there is no method of keeping anybody off the reservation, white society and all of its influences has easy access. That's why the Inn of the Mountain Gods was built. It was already being designed in the 1930s because they already knew that there was going to be a lot of non-Indians wanting to come on this reservation. So they thought about the Inn of the Mountain Gods to keep them in one area to watch over them. So we built the Inn of the Mountain Gods to keep a watch over them.

We have been told that because there can be no border enforcement, outsiders come and cut the wood, take your cattle, sell your cattle. We don't worry about that kind of stuff because every time they take ten cows, fifteen come back. Every time we lose a child, there's always two or three born. Understand? For every cow that drops on the ground and dies, there's three or four more cows born. We balance it out ourselves, all the time. If you get too many, then a predator comes in and kills a little bit off so the others can live. See? That's why they're there. To keep things in balance. Just like turkeys. You get a whole flock of turkeys. Turkeys carry diseases. If you get too many, a couple of coyotes take the weak out.

You talk about balance and harmony. The large number of youths of today are creating an imbalance. How is that going to correct itself?[5] Probably the "man upstairs" is going to take care of that for us because it comes from the family. It's all within. What's happening nowadays is that twelve-year-old girls are having babies already. A kid raising a kid. How can we control that? There's a lot of different ideas about how to control it, but it depends on the person. If that's what they want.

Do the young girls who participate in the puberty ceremony know the ancestral language? If not, how do you get information across to them. No. We tell them in Apache and then state it to them in English also. That's how it's done. That's the only way we can do it. Some girls understand, but very little. Like I said, the language comes from the home. It doesn't come from the classroom. It doesn't come from a tape on a machine. It comes from the home itself, from morning until night. You sit down at a table. The most important table is in the morning—the breakfast table. That's where most conversations come up.

Is there anything lost by the girls only understanding English? Nothing is lost. Everything is already written down. How can it be lost? The puberty ceremony is already written down too. Look on the Internet. How can we lose it? We're not going to lose anything, but we change. *Is the ceremony significant to her when it's taught in English?* Sometimes. Like I said, there's always that balance. Everybody says we're going to lose this, we're going to lose that, but we can't lose it when it's already written. There's no more secrets. It's already done. You've got to have hope. Hope is the biggest word of all. His son, my son, they're the hope for the future. It might not be the Apache language, but it's what's in the big tipi. Performing it and making use of it. That's our hope. Still actually putting the big tipi up—that's our hope. When that tipi lays on the ground, and stays there, then there's no more hope for us. When it fell [in 2004], I put it back up. I was head man. I had the responsibility for it. I put it back up. That's hope. That's a chance to keep living. Not leaving it lay on the ground and not putting it back up.

When it lays on the ground and doesn't get back up, then there's no more hope. It's gone. The wind comes in and buries you. There's always hope. You have to believe in that. Once you lose hope then you're not a whole person anymore. A piece of you got torn off. A piece of you just got taken off. Torn out of you.

Do you see the influence of the white society today not being countered by influences at home? Do you agree that the influence might go back several generations to the boarding-school experience of their grandparents or great-grandparents?[6] Yes. It's had a big impact. I never went to boarding school but my parents threatened to send me to West Point. They had an orphanage in Mescalero. My mom used to take me over there to scare me. "This is where you'll end up at." And it was dirty, smelled like pee, kids were running around with dirty diapers, never taken care of, sores all over them. That's what I saw back in the '60s.

Back in the '50s and '60s they had a big epidemic of pregnancy here. A lot of the ladies got pregnant and they didn't want their kids. They also had a big epidemic of venereal disease here. Killed off a lot of kids and killed off a lot of mothers. That's how come you have a lot of defects in kids too. And then they had an epidemic of women going onto the air force [nearby Holloman Air Force Base] and bringing men here and having kids. They didn't want them. Some of them were half-black, some of them were half-white, and some of them were half-Mexican. So what they did was that they pushed the kids away, into the orphanage. Left them there until they got adopted off the reservation. And most of them that got adopted off the reservation were by the people of Holloman Air Force. So they got shipped off to the service anyway. It was bad for us.

What do you see as the future of the tribe? Do you see the tribe thriving, do you see it holding its own? We are talking about the next twenty-five to fifty years. Do you see it going up or down? It's flexible. One day it's up, one day it's down. Everything is like that. A lot of people's futures are like that. It's a roller coaster. Like these mountains. They come up and go down. Sometimes you have to hit rock bottom before you can get back up to the top. A lot of tribes hit rock bottom with their finances and their culture. They feel like they're torn apart but then they come back up. That's just the way it is. I can predict all I want but I'm only one person. Some people can't see beyond their noses sometime. Some of these people are too stuck to say anything. You really don't know them until you live with them. I have lived here all my life and I know these people. Some are stuck right here and that's it. Me, I look further up.

My kids are the future. So we have hope. That's the big word. Hope is the future. Even if we have one person still standing at Mescalero in existence, we have hope. I don't care if it's an ugly old man or an ugly old woman, we still have hope. It's like in our Apache stories. Man walked around the earth for a long time without a woman. Then woman came about and he had hope. Reproduction. White Painted Woman is included in that. That's how she became—in that reproduction. Man came first in Apache stories. You haven't heard that part yet. There was a lot before White Painted Woman came to us. She came to us because we had a group of people that needed help. There's no other tribe besides us that has twelve tipi poles. There's no other tribe that has White Painted Woman.[7] The Mescalero people started the peyote first here. Not the Mexicans, but the Mescalero people. Some man came from Oklahoma to learn the songs and he took the bundle and went that way. Instead of going around, he went backward. My great-grandmother told my grandmother when it comes back here, there will be no more peyote. It will disappear. And it's getting there, very close. So now you know that.

The people who say there's no future have already given up. Understand? But there is hope. Like I said, if there is just one Apache man or one Apache woman still standing here at Mescalero, then that's our hope. That's how we survived all these years. We have hope. Our children.

If you had all the resources you can think of at your disposal, what would you do to fix the problems on the reservation? I'd have everybody smile every day. It's true. If you look at it, people walk around, don't say hello, don't say how are you doing. We're so small. We don't live in a city. City people only do that. City people pass you and don't say anything. But here, why not say good morning and have a good morning. Up here at Cow Camp everybody says good morning. I love it. Even in my own household, I couldn't say that to my wife because she's just that way. She was raised in the white man's world. "So what? Who gives a shit about that day?" Something like that could be her answer. So I don't say it anymore. I say to my kids, "Hey, how are you doing? Good morning." And they say, "Good morning." And it comes from them. "You have a good day." "Thanks, Dad." That's what keeps me living. That's what keeps me going. Just to say that. When I was teaching at the elementary school I would stand at the bus every morning and greet those kids. "Hey, how are you doing?" Most of them have alcoholic families and they wake up to drinking. They wake up to no breakfast. But for someone to say, "Good morning. You have a good day," that's all it takes for them to have a good day. And a smile on their face. It makes the whole world. When I taught at the high school I saw a kid who was coming out of his shoes. And one day we were outside drawing and I was looking at him and everybody was teasing him because his shoes were coming off him. That's all he had. I started praying, telling God that if tomorrow he didn't have any different shoes, I would buy him some. "Please help him." The kid came back the next day and had brand new shoes on. And I was so happy; all I could say was "Thank you." It makes a believer out of you. That's a big issue. You can't take belief away from anybody. It's hope. My son is hope.

Do you ever see despair? All the time. *Do you ever despair?* Sometimes. Not very often. That's human nature. I push despair aside and keep going. I've got to. I can't sit there and think about it too much.

If you could summarize this whole interview, what would you say? It's hope. Hope for the future of the tribe. Hope for the government to get out of here. And give us our air space back so we can breathe. It's the politics. Politics has a big play on our reservation. Internal politics. Sometimes we have a good leader. Sometimes we don't have a good leader.

—April 14, 2008

TESTIMONY OF DEPREE SHADOWWALKER

I am the oldest child of Margaret B. Fields and Francis Neil Smith. I want to be called Depree Shadowwalker. Shadowwalker is my Indian name. In Apache it's "walk shadow in," but I had to anglicize it so it became Shadowwalker. Depree is a nickname and we have a long history of giving everybody nicknames.

I was born in Mescalero on May 26, 1961. I'm not married and I have no children but I'd like to raise some, to have some other little renegades running around. I'm forty-seven years old. If you grew up here in Mescalero and you're part of this culture, you are Chiricahua, Mescalero, Lipan Apache. If you look at my dad's blood, he was registered as half Chiricahua and I'm a quarter. But if you look at our lineage, we have several generations over here. My dad and his family grew up speaking three languages—English, Spanish, and Apache. They knew more Apache than they did of any other language and it is their culture and heritage. Everything that came through their life built who they are today, came from being Apache. But if you look at the way the government assigns things, you're only so much Indian because that way they don't have to assist you or hold to their treaties.[1]

I have a long history of using my original name, which is Debra Marie Smith, and it's still a part of Depree Shadowwalker, but whenever I got pulled over by cops they never thought it was my name because I wasn't married. My last name, Smith, sounded too illegal. So I was always getting harassed by the law. Within administrations, Debra Smith never had a problem getting jobs, getting positions anywhere off the reservation. When I changed my name to Depree Shadowwalker I have had the hardest time getting any type of position off the reservation. I can't get into positions I could have gotten into very easily as Debra Smith.

Were you raised here on the reservation? This is home. I know all the smells here. I know where everything is. Everybody except the younger generation knows me, although I can't remember who they are. I spent my early years, on and off, at Mescalero because my mom and dad divorced when I was four. My dad was my main caretaker when I was growing up, and that's how I ended up Apache, that's how I know about cultures. When my sister was born, my mom and dad got a divorce, so my sister has more of the Spanish culture than I do. She was raised by my grandmother, Candaleria Fields, off the reservation. My dad spoke Apache. He would come here and go to the ceremonies and attend all the functions. The Mescaleros and everybody knew me because I was a baby. When you are a little kid, the world is yours. Half my family was up here and the other half was in Tularosa.

Tell us about life on the reservation today as compared to how you remember it. It's changing. When I was growing up, for one thing, everybody took care of the kids. It didn't matter whose kids you were, somebody always took care of you. It didn't matter where you were, if there was an adult there you didn't have to worry. They watched over you. They made sure you ate. That's not happening now. I hear, and I've asked several other people, that there are kids growing up who have nothing to eat, their parents are never home, the relatives never come and check on them, they have no place to go. That's a big difference.

When did it change? I came back from working on my Ph.D. in 2005. I left in 2003. *In 2003 people still looked after the children?* As far as I could tell, especially among the older people. That was a part of their culture. I always hung around with the older people. They kept family traditions, the Apache language and values alive. When I came back, a lot of them had passed on. I just found out about it recently. The rumors fly around the reservation all the time and most of the time they are not true, but this time I brought it up to a couple of medicine people and they said it was true.

What caused this change? What didn't cause this change? The dominant culture that you see on TV is influential. I was telling Ellen Bigrope[2] at the cultural museum that what I think has happened is that we started to discriminate against our own people. We have had to hire educated people—outsiders from off the reservation—from various locations. They come in already with a prejudice against us. They instill an institutional-type prejudice in administrative policies. We get that same feeling of oppression again from the dominant society. When we go off and get educated, we don't see the difference. We think, "OK, here comes an educated person. This person knows me. They're going to discriminate against me even more." And sometimes we Apaches do that. You come back and you say, "We don't want this educated person who knows me like the back of my hand to get into this or that position because they might hurt me even further." So, it's hard to hire our own educated people because we are unconsciously afraid that they will discriminate against us even more because they know our family.

You can't fire all the white people and get them off the reservation. No, because they're educated. They have more network connections than we do and that's why they're in the position they're in. But, what we can do is on-the-job training for the people who are here. Slowly move them up into those positions. Have a phase-out phase for the other people who don't belong here. The enterprises here are supposed to have been developed for us.

Would you like to work on the reservation? Yes, or in universities. I have applied to be a Native American professor, I have applied for teaching positions here on the reservation, I applied to all the branch universities, UTEP, Eastern New Mexico, etcetera.

As an adult, when there was no work here on the reservation, I would leave and go look for work. When I'd get in trouble off the reservation, I would come back home. Getting in trouble means to me that I didn't have a job or emotionally couldn't handle what was going on out there. Then I'd come back home to recuperate.

What are your qualifications for employment? I was in the military for six years, ten months, and I forgot the number of days. I was a combat medic and got out as an E-5. I was also a laboratory specialist and I have an associate's degree in electronics, which is my bread and butter. I usually fall back on that one because everybody needs a technician. My bachelor's degree started off in architecture, and when I saw I wasn't going to get very far in that because of the good-old-boys' club, I fell back on my second major, which was fine arts, ceramics. My master's degree is in education and learning technologies. I entered this field when I was working here at the school in the old buildings. And then I went off to get my Ph.D., thinking I could do something. Now the most I can do is finish my degree.

So you say Apaches are also discriminating against Apaches and prefer to join the outsiders rather than help another Apache get ahead. Yes. *Is that only among the educated who come back?* No. It's also the ones who stay because they're thinking, "At least this white person doesn't know my family history, maybe they will give me a chance. But this Indian person, a tribal member, knows my whole family history and they might discriminate against me even further."

After I got my master's degree I was traumatized. I read something about us Indians and the boarding schools. And then it dawned on me. No wonder. I gave up my own culture to learn, to get an education, to get a good job, and be successful. It didn't happen. It still hasn't happened. But I don't want to leave here. I'm almost fifty. I'd rather be poor, living here, where I know where things are, like the mountains, the smells. I tried to find everything that I grew up with someplace else and even though I'll be poor living here, I'd rather live here.

Can you suggest a solution to the situation of Apaches going away, getting educated, and coming back to problems? Mentors. You have to have people who will mentor you back into the community. You have to get reeducated to the community. You have to come here for the summer and work, be around the people, attend the feasts [puberty ceremonies], have the opportunities. There's the informal education and the formal education, and we have to separate the two. There are people on the reservation who have no formal education but they are Ph.D.'s in the culture, in the language, and everything else. They just don't have a degree. That's the type of mentor you need. Look, nowadays there are hardly any activists. Back in my aunt's day there were people who were activists. They engaged in the politics, they engaged in the government, they got things done, they got the Chiricahua land grant that was supposed to fund our scholarship money. They didn't have an education. None of them went to law school. Some of them didn't even have associates' degrees. Some of them didn't even finish high school, and yet they were able to create government policy and create opportunities for the tribe. That's not happening now.

We are getting educated now just to follow the dominant society, and the dominant society is educating for cogs in the wheel, not for activists. I asked someone why he thought that had happened. He was an activist and gave me an example. He said, "I remember we were trying to lobby the United States for something and were trying to contact one of the really high officials in Washington, D.C. Couldn't get on his schedule to talk to him formally." He figured out that the official had to ride the subway that goes to the Pentagon. He got on that subway train, saw the official and sat down next to him and started talking to him. He had a whole thirty-minute ride and finally got the issue heard by this prominent person, and got the bill passed. That type of thinking outside the box doesn't occur anymore. Most people give up before they get to that point.

You said that when a person leaves the reservation, becomes educated, and comes back, they need a connection to the tribe; for example, mentors. But it's not happening. Right. It's dying out. *You also said that when you come back as an educated person and you try to get a job here, nobody will hire you because of the competition.* And also because they, the Indian people, feel threatened that you're going to take their job. It's very complicated.

Still, you came back. Explain that pull. I can see the stars at night. I can feel the wind. I know all the animals. I know all the plants. People say "Hi" to you, even if they are mad at you. I tried to find other places that had all the other things like the Mescalero mountains, water, stars, and I'd walk there and it felt empty. It felt like I was just a visitor. I'm attracted to red earth and so I went to Moab [Utah] where they have all that red earth, and it was so beautiful but I felt like a man on the moon. Everywhere I go there is beautiful land, the earth is soft and there's all this different quality—the beach—and stare across the ocean and hear the waves. But then I come home for five minutes and ahhhh. I'm home.

You said that the tribe needs educated Apaches because otherwise you have white people coming in, being managers, and taking advantage. On the other hand you have the educated Apache who leaves, comes back, and the tribe doesn't utilize this educated person. Whose fault is that? The tribe's. Some people say it's the individual who has the education and doesn't do anything about it because he gets knocked down if he does. The tribe is saying, "Get educated, leave, so the rest of us who are not educated can have a job."

Sounds like the tribe is at war with itself. No, they want to be like the dominant culture. They think that being businesslike is going to help the tribe survive, but it hasn't. It never has and it never will. What's going to end up happening is that we're going to lose our reservation. We're on the verge of losing our casino because of the influence of the dominant culture. Let me give you an example. When I left the reservation as a young girl, I didn't have a concept of time. I also had a lot more intuitive powers than what I do now. I was a lot stronger physically, mentally, and spiritually before I learned about time. I joined the National Guard and learned about time, because you hurry up and wait. So I started to gauge things. I took that idea of time and started to learn more about it. I learned time is linear. In the Apache way, time is not segmented into seconds and minutes. Time is circular; it's a rhythm, a motion to follow. I brought linear time back to the reservation and others misinterpreted it.

In the army I learned how to watch the clock. I never knew that. That's how I got in trouble at my last job. I told them I have a learning disability, that I'm not very good at watching the clock. Will you please excuse me until I get a handle on this new schedule? They didn't believe me.

Is the clock a symbol to you of the white society in providing structure and form, a symbol of conformity? Yes. There's different types of structure and form. If you build a square house, that's structure and form, right? If you build a tipi, that's structure and form too, but it's a different shape, right? They both house people, but they're different structures. But the only structure anybody knows is the house. The dominant society says you are civilized if you live in a square house. If you're really, really rich, you can have the craziest looking house in the whole world.

The clock was just an analogy for business. We were talking about how the tribe has to be more businesslike. There are enterprises we can start that can be businesslike but we need to make accommodations for our culture. It can't be an imitation of the way the white society does business. It has to be an original way of doing business that has to be traditional and adaptive. When we do these language workshops we open it with prayer. Look at the way the white society is now. You can't even pray in the schools. In the traditional way, all societies opened things with prayer. Any negotiation was with prayer. "Please help us work on this issue that we have brought forth. Come into this room and be at this table." There was a spirituality component that's not in corporate business. They open up with an idea of Manifest Destiny.[3]

The tribe is not a dominant society culture or organization. But the tribe has to be a corporation to survive. There are other indigenous models available but we get stuck with the idea of doing things the dominant society way. But we don't have to do it that way. I got into an argument with one of my co-workers in the IT department, a very young white man, on the reservation who said there should be no tribe, there should be no reservation, they should be incorporated into the dominant society, tribal members should have preference at any enterprise, etc. Nobody complains about corporations or millionaires and what they do with their money, who they hire, or how they handle their business.

Who complains about the tribe? Everybody who's not a tribal member complains that we are so rich, look at this wonderful house they gave you, you don't even have to work, the government pays you, every misconception possible. The most outrageous thing I ever heard was that in Alamogordo a high school teacher had this myth that Apache girls were promiscuous and the way they could tell was because they pierced their ears. So any Apache girl who had her ears pierced was promiscuous.

What are the problems you see that are related to the tribe's relationship to the government or the dominant culture? Our hospital has gone to pot. They have less and less staff. I've gone there when it's been closed. I just wanted to get my records so I could tend to a medical condition—a chiropractor in Alamogordo. They told me to stop off and get my x-rays so they could look at my x-rays and we could see if there were any changes. The hospital was closed. There's no emergency room although they say there is one. They used to pay for it if our hospital wasn't open and you went to another hospital. They used to pay the bill but now they're not paying the bill and they're not telling you. So, you can get bad credit because the collection agency sends you a notice that they're going to ruin your credit.

When did this start happening? I just started noticing this year. And it's not the people up there because they are nice. There are a lot of tribal members who still work there and they still do the same job that they've always done.

Tell me about the drug problem among Apaches. My cousin had her feast [puberty ceremony] and was well versed in Apache culture. She went off to go to school. We ended up at the same university. She was working on her Ph.D. and her master's simultaneously and then she got hooked up with crystal meth in a university setting. Everything went downhill from there. She never completed her degrees, she's been to prison a couple of times. She was going to be a kinesiologist. She was bright and was doing good research and had good mentors at the university who were helping her do her degrees simultaneously. She had so much potential. But that drug—when it gets hold of you . . . She never wanted to come back. She would get frustrated and say that she didn't want to come back here because nobody among the educated people was ever supportive of her. She decided that she could make a better living off the reservation and at least have some type of support. She's in prison for stealing her dead sister's identity and was writing illegal checks. Something like that.

What about the future? That's scary. It looks like what's going to happen is that we won't have a reservation. Already outsiders just wander in, take trees. They come in, they go fishing in our ponds that are stocked for tribal members, but the fish aren't there for them because the people come in and fish. They don't get permission, they don't care, they act like they're not doing anything wrong. They shoot off their guns, they leave their trash. We're not going to have a reservation. We may have to give up our land to pay debts that we incur. That's what happened in the east. A lot of those tribes don't have a reservation anymore because they voted the wrong people into council. They get into there and our government isn't set up with checks and balances. So we become a monarchy that can be destroyed.

The president and the council members say they're going to change policies, but once they get in there, they like that power. There's a difference between having no education and not doing anything productive for the tribe and having no education and building policy and helping business. The Navajos are looking at governance that's built on culture and not so much on the dominant society's model. Our leaders and people in office should take a look at that.

If the dominant society had stayed out, off the reservation, would things be different now? Yes. Real different. It would probably be like it was when I was growing up. *Better?* Yes. But, we have to deal with each other. When we are here with ourselves we have to learn to get along, we have to learn to help each other out because we are all we have. But when you let other people in from the outside, then you have to learn how they play the game in order to even be included. But they don't play by the rules. Look at Enron. Also the invisibility of being Indian. Apparently there's no history of Indian children being forced to school in New Mexico history without their parents' permission. When I took a history course, there's no evidence of our tribe in it. How come our tribe isn't in here? We're here. It's no different now. Still, it's the invisibility.[4]

If the U.S. government decided that this tribe had so many problems, could they take the land? They would take the land like they did in the east. They would privatize everything so they could tax it. They would take the land and sell it. *How can they legally do that?* Because we would be unable to manage it. That's how they took things from us in the first place. They say, "You can't handle what we gave you." *Isn't there a treaty prohibiting that?* Those are the old days. Nobody adheres to those things because "we're all Americans now." So there is no such thing as an Apache anymore.

What makes up a tribe? Is it just the reservation or also the language, the songs, the prayers? A lot of the tribes that have been disintegrated, like that tribe in the east, have privatized land. They still call it a reservation but it's cornfields. They don't have their language and they argue that you can still be Indian without the language. It's kind of like drinking a Coke. When you add ice to it and don't drink it, it loses its fizzle, the ice melts, it dilutes the Coke and it no longer tastes like Coke. It's still legally Coke. You can't be a Chiricahua Apache without the language. Every tribe that has held onto their language knows so much more about their culture because all of the influences of that culture from time immortal are embedded in that language. For example, it may seem just like it's a word for a stick but that stick—all these little letters that came together—are not just a word for a stick. It's all the little sounds that blossom out into this whole encyclopedic knowledge that comes out here, that you can't access without the language. Once you lose the language, you lose the meaning of the songs, the prayers. They just become rhetoric. Like Latin in the church.

Do you see that happening to your tribe? Yes. There are people now who won't speak Apache, not because they don't understand it or never spoke it before, but because they haven't used it enough to have a dialogue or feel comfortable speaking it. A lot of my cousins are that way. *Who are they going to talk to in Apache out in the world?* That's why they didn't teach me. I didn't learn Apache or Spanish. Is the goal to go out into the world to succeed or is the goal to maintain tribal culture here?

When all the grandmothers die, who will pass on the culture? We're already losing our culture; the mores and the values aren't being passed on. *How would you preserve the culture?* You have to honor it. You can't let the outside people say it isn't any good.

Sounds like you are pessimistic about the future of the tribe. Well, I'm not willing to go down without a fight.

—February 25, 2008

TESTIMONY OF ALFRED LAPAZ

For the record, my name is Alfred G. LaPaz. I was born here in Mescalero in 1948. I'm Mescalero and Lipan Apache. I have lived here at Mescalero pretty much all my life. I graduated from Tularosa High School in 1967. That same year I traveled to San Francisco by train by myself and went to school in a little town called Kentfield in the fall of 1967 and 1968. I stayed there, met a lot of people, made some friends and traveled to different reservations while I was there. After that I came home here to Mescalero and stayed here, got married in 1969.

My wife is a quarter Mescalero, her father is Art Blazer and he spent a big portion of his life here at Mescalero. His wife's name is Leeta Blazer, a tribal member, and her family lived here at Mescalero for a big portion of their life also. I'm still married, going on thirty-nine years. Next year will be forty years. We have three children and ten grandchildren. I enjoy every one of them. *Is your wife's family part of the Blazer's Mill history?*[1] Yes, the father and grandfather had a lot to do with the Blazer Mill.

In 1969 I got involved in law enforcement and went to work with the tribal conservation department, which was a program that was just starting here in Mescalero. I worked for a little over a year and then there was a position that came open with the tribal police department. I applied and was hired. I worked for a short time and then the Bureau of Indian Affairs [BIA] law enforcement had a position open. I was fortunate enough to get on with them and I stayed there for many years. I transferred to northern California on the Hupa reservation, where I worked with the Hupa group and Yurok tribes. I lived right on the coast in Klamath, California. We lived there for a little over two years and then we moved back here. At that time the federal government was going through an RIF[2] and I was accepted in a position, but during my transfer my position had closed, so I ended up without a job just for a short time.

The Ruidoso Police Department hired me right away as soon as I got back. I worked with the Ruidoso Police Department for over two years. Then the BIA law enforcement had another position, I applied, and got back into government service because I had already done so many years there. I stayed with the federal government for thirty years and retired as a captain. I was offered the position of director of security at the Inn of the Mountain Gods. I was there for six years. I resigned from there. At the same time I was hired as the director of security I put my name in for the Mescalero Tribal Council. I was elected and served for eight consecutive years.

What does the Tribal Council do, and what are the powers of the Tribal Council? The tribal constitution is the law of the reservation. We have the tribal president. The administration consists of ten people, the president, vice president, and eight council members. Right now I am the secretary for the council.

How does the Tribal Council work? When I got on the Tribal Council the late Sara Misquez was the president. After that Mark Chino was elected. I was appointed as part of the executive committee at that time. Now Carleton Naiche-Palmer is president. This is like my fourth term. Each administration has its own way of doing things. They are different. But basically everything is the same as far as the tribal constitution goes, but the way they work things is a little bit different. They approach things from a different point sometimes. I was able to adjust and work well with all three administrations.

When a decision is to be made, do all the councilors have to agree with it, along with the president? Or, are there times when just the president decides? What is the decision-making process? The president can make certain decisions on his own. He has the power to do that. But the power lies within the council. The council has the power to overturn the president's decision. It has to be a majority vote. The president cannot vote on anything. The vice president also cannot vote on anything but he can break a tie. We discuss issues, sometimes a long deliberation, and then we vote.

Are you responsible for any particular area with the Tribal Council? There are several committees within the administration. The eight council members serve on these committees. I currently serve as chair for one of these committees.

Let's go back to the thirty years that you were a police officer. Was most of that time on the reservation here? The majority of it was here in Mescalero but I have traveled many places to work. I have worked in Arizona in the Window Rock area, on the Navajo Reservation also. In California, Minnesota, and Montana. That short break in the middle was with the city of Ruidoso. So, actually I have worked thirty-two years. I have been exposed to so much during my tenure as a law enforcement officer. My relationship with my people got pretty close where I was able to work with a lot of the older and younger people—meaning young adults to teenagers in high school. I feel I've contributed something good, and that makes me feel good.

What was some of the work that you did? I feel I've always been there to serve my people—alcohol and drugs and these kinds of things. I got to where I was able to gain the trust of my people. I really enjoyed that because I felt like I contributed a lot. *Are you talking about teenagers?* Not just teenagers, but the tribe as a whole.

What did you advise? I tell them that if they get a chance to go off the reservation, to go to school, to live, take advantage of it. That way you'll know firsthand what it's like to live among the white man, to see what their world is like. And if you go to school off the reservation, learn whatever you can, gain all that knowledge and then you can bring that back home to your people. That's some of the things that I told a lot of people I talked to, but other times they went into other things, personal things. That's some of the basic things that are important, their education, some of the things that I expressed to them, for them to succeed in what they're doing in their lives.

Do they take your suggestions to heart? What I like about that is that when I talk to people, a lot of times they will come back and say, "You know the discussion we had? It has put a change in my life and I am doing better." It makes me feel good, like I did something for them. So I tell them that my door is always open. They can still come to me anytime they want. I'll always make time for them. There's a lot of people that don't have anybody to talk to and for some reason they will not open up to their parents, or to their relatives.

You see life on the reservation from two approaches—one from law enforcement and one as an elected official. One thing that I like and I feel that I was fortunate, is that our tribe, our people—when I talk to a lot of people nowadays and even when I was still in law enforcement—I felt like I could comfortably say, "Hey, you don't need to tell me this because I was there." I went through the same hardship that some of our people went through in the past when times were still tough. I remember just vaguely when people still lived in tents, probably in the '50s. We had outside restrooms, there was no inside running water. Very few people had electricity. In the mornings I would get up, go outside to get wood chips to build a fire. I walked about one hundred yards to the road with two buckets. Dipped water out of the spring and brought it back. At that time I was still a young person but it's how far back I can remember. It makes me feel proud because I was able to live a part of this kind of life. Things are different now. I can say that I can still remember some of the things that we had to do.

I spent a lot of time with my aunt, Pauline LaPaz, when I was growing up. She is one of the nicest persons anyone could ever meet. She was the one who would do more for us cousins when we were growing up. She spoiled all her nieces and nephews.

Going back to your dual perspective, you see today's problems with the young people—the drugs, the alcohol, the teenage pregnancies, the truancy, the dropout record. Is that the influence of the dominant society coming onto the reservation? Well, I see it from different sides. One of the most important things is alcohol and lack of jobs.

When I was in BIA law enforcement it seemed like the different branches of the BIA and the community worked closer together than they do now. I feel that the BIA is trying to phase out slowly and you can see it. They are lacking in a lot of responsibilities. They have a trust responsibility to the tribe and they are not following through.

One of our interviewees wanted the government off the reservation. Said, "Let us handle it ourselves. Let us do it ourselves. Give us the money. We'll run the show ourselves. Get off our reservation." What do you think about that? I think the government has a trust responsibility and we can't let them go. One tribe has worked out something that got rid of all the government on its reservation, except one. It's the superintendent. Got rid of all the BIA and leave the superintendent here, who is BIA. He can be responsible in continuing incoming funds from the government to the tribe. The superintendent can oversee the distribution of funding for different programs. We can get our own roads program. We can get our own social services. We can get our own different programs. And the government funding will continue to come in through the superintendent and we can figure out how much money will be allocated for different programs.

What about the tribal police? How many do you have and are they able to be effective with the resources they have? You mean right now? The tribal police was slowly faded out and the federal government took over law enforcement. Right now our law enforcement people are federal, BIA. There is the tribal conservation department who act as the tribal police. They have certain responsibilities. They can be assigned to certain things in law enforcement. Right now part of their requirements is to go through the BIA law enforcement academy. So we don't have any tribal police—just the tribal conservation officers. I think they changed their title to "Tribal Law Enforcement Officers." Our law enforcement is all BIA. We used to have an FBI agent who was directly here with us but he retired so now we have a BIA special investigator who is assigned to our area. That's who is down here now.

Law enforcement is a big problem because we don't have a detention center. That really creates a problem for our people. We have people who are sent off to detention centers or minimum security prisons where a lot of them are exposed to a lot of bad things and it's brought back to our homes.

Being the head of law enforcement, at one time I went through the detention center at least six times with different people from Washington, from Albuquerque—the chief law enforcement office from BIA—and every time we went through there they said, "Well, we have the money appropriated for this and you are going to have a new detention center." It never happened and to this day we still don't have one. I got out eight years ago and there's still no detention center. I have met with a lot of people, including Hillary Clinton up in Washington and I talked with her for some time. I addressed some of our concerns here and some of the big problems that our people are facing now—housing, health care, education, law enforcement, etc.

At that time she was very concerned with IHS so we talked a lot about it. That's when our hospitals were cutting down on hours and it was starting to have an effect on services. They have always had twenty-four-hour services here. It got to where people couldn't be seen after certain hours. They came to the door at one minute after ten and were told, "Well, I'm sorry but you have to go to Ruidoso." Things like that. So, I addressed these with Senator Clinton and she told us that she would do something about this. We met her about three years go. *She was going to do something as a senator?* Yes, as a senator.

Do you have any idea how to fix these problems? The tribe has always been up against situations that could have an effect on the people, the land, the resources. The people put their trust into the elected officials and have given them the responsibility to address the issues. But there are times when the Tribal Council needs the support of the people to address the issues. The Mescalero Apaches are a strong people who can overcome a lot of these issues. That's why we are still here. We have grown stronger and have a better outlook and can move forward with changes but are still able to maintain our tradition and culture.

Some tribal members worry that the more you play the white man's game, the more like the white man you become and the less Apache you become. If so, your choice is between a rock and hard place. If you play the white man's game, you lose your Apache-ness. If you remain Apache, you also lose. What do you think of that? I believe that the white man has been trying to get the Native American to play his game from as far back as I can remember. The native people resisted for as long as they could, until they got overpowered and could not do anything anymore.

Today there are still people out there that feel aggression for the hardship that their people had to go though—slaughter, warfare, hatred, and disease. But in order for our people to survive and strive to live a long life, we must accept the changes of the modern world.

I believe it is very important for our elected tribal officials to work together. It takes teamwork to get things done and, most importantly, I think it takes the support of the people, the tribe, understanding, and so forth.

In order for the tribe to be successful in business enterprises, bringing money into the tribe and being able to offer programs for the people, does the tribe have to become like white society to get things accomplished? To go forward? That's a hard question for me. Like I said, you cannot forget where you came from. Your culture, your traditions, your beliefs and your medicine people have to be there. But at the same time we must have to be able to meet the challenges in the white man's world.

How do you achieve both? Well, I talked to my people, especially young people, and said that you need to go to school. Education is the main thing. You need to go as far as you can. Go to college. Learn all these things and someday you can return to your homelands and become great leaders.

Insofar as tradition is concerned, is preserving the language a key to preserving the culture? Preserving the language is part of it. Believing in what you were taught has a lot to do with it. In the home and the way you were brought up. When I was working as a police officer, for many years I worked with my uncle. The old man taught me a lot, a lot of good things, a lot of good ways. If our people can learn that and keep it, I think that will be one the greatest things, along with our language. I think it's a possibility because I think of our Head Start program. They have a time in there when they teach the little kids our language and different ways of our people. I think that's where they need to start, at that age. *And it needs to be supplemented in the home also?* Yes, parents should be encouraged to teach their children, talk to them about the language, teach them and let them know where we came from, our people. And even some of the suffering that our people had to go through.

At the Inn of the Mountain Gods they have a short class during orientation for employment. We have a lot of people who come from all over, from across the country to enjoy the Inn of the Mountain Gods. A lot of people will come in and ask questions about the tribe. Who is the president? How old is the reservation? How big is it? Also, we have a lot of non-Indian employees out there who know nothing about it. Our Human Resources Department has now made it a requirement to attend a session on Apache history. So, when people come in and ask questions, they will get answers.

What resources does the tribe have that bring in money? Right now the Inn of the Mountain Gods is the main resource for the tribe. We have four places under that umbrella. We have the Inn of the Mountain Gods Resort and Casino, the travel center, the ski area, and the hunting lodge. Take for example the hunting lodge. They have sold all their permits for the year already, amounting to about $150,000.

What do you see happening to the tribe in the next fifty years? There's a big future for our tribe. We need to educate our young people; it's up to them. Right now I think we're at the point where we need to change our people and get them to understand that to make this happen we all need to work together. I think the Apache people have always been a strong, strong tribe. I believe the Mescalero tribe has a bright future. We have the best land in the state of New Mexico, in the southwest, all over. So, with that I'm looking forward to having a good future. Maybe some day we'll have a native running this country.

—June 11, 2008

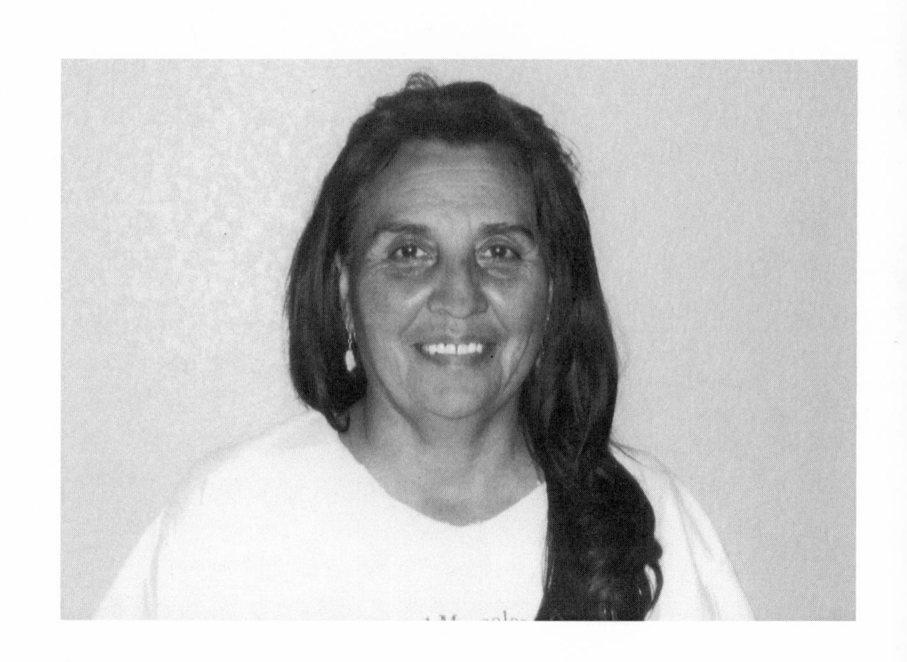

TESTIMONY OF DEBI MARTINEZ

My birth name is Debra Kaye Blaylock. Blaylock is my maiden name. My married name now is Martinez. Everyone knows me as Debi. Some people call me Debra. My mother is Elbys Naiche Hugar and my father was Clayton Blaylock. My mother is the great-granddaughter of Chief Cochise. Her grandfather was Christian Naiche Sr. and her father was Christian Naiche Jr. So I am the great-great-granddaughter of Cochise. On my father's side, he was Anglo and he was from Cookville, Tennessee. He was in the Air Force, stationed in Alamogordo at Holloman Air Force Base. My mother was out of school and working at the Blind School in Alamogordo.[1] She and my dad met at the movies in Alamogordo in 1950. He was working at Holloman with the Man in Space program with the chimpanzees. He was one of the individuals that trained Ham, the first monkey in space and trained many other monkeys after that for flights into space. He was never sent to any war.

My dad also worked with Colonel Stapp, the individual who rode the fastest sled. It was just a sled on a track. There was a force behind it and it slowed down in a pool of water. They did it at Holloman. They have the sled and a portion of the track up at the Space Hall of Fame in Alamogordo.

I was born in 1954 at Holloman Air Force Base. There's seven of us children. I'm second born. I have an older sister and five younger brothers and I have four half-brothers and sisters—two half-brothers and two half-sisters. My mother and father had separated and divorced and remarried.

From Holloman we moved off base to Tularosa, but my dad was still employed there. I remember telling my mom some stories that I remembered from when I was very young. My first memory is that we lived in a white house and there was a driveway. I walked down the driveway and crossed the road to an irrigation ditch with a board across it. I would walk across the board to the fence. There was a donkey in there. I would pick up the apricots that fell on the ground and feed them to the donkey.

When I told her that story, she said I was only two years old at that time. Now I can just picture a two-year-old doing that.

We lived in Tularosa for maybe two years and then we moved up to the reservation. I remember the first structure that we lived in. It was a canvas tent. We moved in the summertime. Throughout the summer my father and my mom's brother, Preston, were building a one-room home for us to live in during the wintertime. It's in the area of the reservation they call Broken Arrow. It wasn't at Whitetail. I remember we had rabbits, rabbits, and more rabbits. My dad and my uncle would kill the rabbits and my mom would cook them. I remember eating rabbit meat. We had our own garden and grew different kinds of vegetables. We had to pull the weeds and water the garden and make sure the garden was the way it was supposed to be.

I remember living in the tent and I remember the daddy longlegs, the spider. They would be climbing up the wall of the tent and then when they started climbing up the angle of the roof of the tent they would fall down on us. We didn't like that so we would pull the legs off them and put them back on the ground so they wouldn't crawl back up and fall back down on us. At night when my mom turned the lamp off we would cover our heads with the blankets because we didn't want them to crawl in our mouth or ears or in the bed with us.

The tent was probably a 12 × 14. I remember three beds in there. My mom and dad slept in one, my sister Joyce and I slept in one, and two of my younger brothers slept in the other bed. During the next summer we were living in the house and I remember my grandmother having supper with us and she told all of us kids, "Now you clean your plates real good because I'm not washing dishes tonight. I'm just putting them back up in the cabinet." My grandmother's name was Alta Treas Naiche. She died when she was sixty years old. I knew her for a very short time and I have very few memories of her. We lost her to pneumonia. My dad had that one-room house built for us. Later on they were moving the Whitetail houses down to Mescalero and so I remember moving into a house that they moved from Whitetail on Broken Arrow Road. I remember my mom coming home from the hospital with a little baby in her arms and it was my brother Dennis. I remember her sitting on the bed crying. At that time I didn't know why but as I grew older I found out that she had twins, Dennis and Janice, and Janice had passed away. She didn't survive. The only two times I remember my mother crying is when Janice died and then when my grandmother passed away. My grandfather moved in with us. He lived with us then. Grandpa Christian.[2]

Tell us about your education. I remember going to a day school. I think they call it Head Start today. It was up at the Mescalero agency. I remember we had little rugs that we put on the floor that we would take a nap on. In the afternoon, right after lunch an Indian man who drove the school bus would come. They would call several names. We would leave and go with him and I would find myself in the dentist's office in Alamogordo. Every time I saw him I would say, "Oh, please, don't call my name."

From that day school I went to the elementary school at Mescalero—kindergarten through sixth grade—and that's the highest grade it went to on the reservation. From there most of the students went to Tularosa High School and a few of them went to Ruidoso High School from seventh through twelfth grades. My seventh grade year I went to the Tularosa Middle School for about one month. I didn't know things were in the works for me to be transferred to an Indian school. Right at this time my mom and dad were going through a divorce and within that first month after school started, my older sister and I were both taken to Albuquerque Indian School. It was a boarding school. I remember crying and telling my dad I didn't want to stay. He told me that I had to. It was about 1967. I was there during seventh and eighth grades. During my freshman year I came back to Mescalero and I attended school at Tularosa High School and then tenth and eleventh grades I went back to the Albuquerque Indian School. When I came home for the summer, my mom [who was living in Apache, Oklahoma] came to visit during the Fourth of July and asked if I wanted to go back to Oklahoma with her and go to school there during my senior year. My sister, Joyce, was already over there. So I talked to my dad about it and he said it was OK with him. So, I packed my bags, left with her, and did my senior year in Apache High School.

Every summer that I returned from school at the Albuquerque Indian School I worked for the youth program in Mescalero. I started in the workforce when I was fifteen years old. My first job was planting trees and watering them for the summer on the reservation. I think it was called the JTPA program back then and was for the young kids who came from low-income families. That was my very first job. I took driver's ed at the Albuquerque Indian School and got my driver's license when I was fifteen. After high school I came back to Mescalero. I met a young man and soon we were married. I continued to work. I worked at the hospital in the Contract Health Department. I also worked at the school as a teacher's aide in Mescalero and Tularosa. I worked as an alcohol and drug counselor. I began that work in the late '70s until today. I have a certificate as a licensed alcohol and drug counselor. You have to be licensed through the State of New Mexico.

Is it difficult to become licensed? I don't think "hard" is the right word. It's time consuming because you have to put years of experience in and put that in your application. You take a test and it goes before the New Mexico Board. Then you're given your certificate and you have to renew it every year.

I went to college at Eastern New Mexico University and I just took the basics like math and English, I took speech and human relations. That was before I started in the counseling field.

I happened to apply for a night monitor job and little did I know that they were guiding me into becoming a counselor. The director at that time was Silas Cochise and his assistant was John Hubbard, and they would tell me that they had a meeting in Albuquerque that they had to go to and that I had to go with them. It was actually a training for counselors. They started taking me along. Pretty soon I started doing groups and before I knew it they had me doing individual counseling. So I have several heroes in my life: my father and, of course, my great-great-grandfather Cochise, my great-grandfather Naiche, my grandfather Christian Naiche Jr., and my mother are first and foremost. In the workforce—I was asked the other day who I attribute my success to—it's to two individuals. They don't know this; I have never told them. It is Silas Cochise and John Hubbard.

I consider Silas Cochise to be my uncle. His mother and my grandfather, Christian, were brother and sister. Her name was Amelia Naiche. So Silas and my mother, Elbys, are first cousins. But I have always known him as Uncle Silas. He was the director of the inpatient rehabilitation center back in 1972 when I started there. John Hubbard was a counselor there. Those two men started me on the road of helping others. I had hit bottom. I had my battle with alcohol. When I started in that field it helped me get stronger and maintain my own sobriety and enjoy life. It's not easy. I think it's worse when you are a drinker and an alcoholic.

I have four daughters. I have my children to think about. I had gone through a divorce so I was a single mother for nine years and I was an alcohol/drug counselor so they put me on the right track. They pulled me out of the gutter and helped me get back on track.

I also attended the Technical Vocational Institute (TVI) in Albuquerque. I took computer classes there and learned how to write programs for businesses to implement in computers as in data collections. For banks, for accounting purposes.

Now you're a tribal judge. Will you tell us a little about that? In the field of alcohol and drugs and being a substance abuse and alcohol counselor, we go through burnout so I left counseling and went to the Inn of the Mountain Gods and became a blackjack dealer. I took the courses and I passed and got the job in the year 2000. I worked there only five months when the chief judge of the Mescalero tribal court—at that time it was Steve Wall—asked me to come see him, so I did. He talked to me about a drug court program that they wanted to implement on our reservation and that they needed a substance abuse counselor to coordinate the program. For the five months that I was a blackjack dealer I was in all this smoke, dealing cards to alcoholics. I didn't like that. I was working late nights and weekends and so this job offer, being 8:00 to 4:30, five days a week, weekends and holidays off, was the perfect job.

What does the tribal court do? The tribal court is basically the judicial system for the tribe. There is a separation of powers from the executive and the Tribal Council. The tribal court handles all the matters of people who break the law on the reservation. The tribal court deals with Indians only, doesn't just have to be Mescalero. As long as they are natives, the court has jurisdiction as long as they break the law on the reservation. They can be an affiliate, married into the tribe, but the court has no jurisdiction over a non-Indian, meaning someone who is white, Mexican, Negro, or Asian. If they are not Native Americans we cannot try them in our court. It would have to be taken to a state court. There are three judges and two alternate judges because sometimes a judge will become disqualified because he or she is related to the people in the court. Everybody is related so somewhere you have to draw the line. Now they tell me that if it's your immediate family, or if it's your uncle's family or your aunt's family, I can't hear those cases, but beyond that I can.

How did you become a judge? I went from a blackjack dealer to the drug court coordinator. That's a treatment program for nonviolent offenders who may have a DUI or they are charged with intoxication or drug abuse. We get them out of jail, get them counseling and jobs and back in their home setting. I did that for seven years. We had an opening for an associate judge. The judge who was there left when her term was up and she didn't reapply. We only had one associate judge and no chief judge at the time. By that time a chief judge had come on board. She was a Navajo and she called me in and talked with me. Many had encouraged me to take the judge's position and I always refused. So, I applied for the position.

Why? One of the things that I saw for myself was that politics can get out of hand. And people can harass and call each other names—things like that. Sometimes it would end up in court. Working with the drug program I wasn't part of tribal court, but I observed what happened there. I never did like politics. I never wanted to be part of politics. I liked what I did in helping people restore their lives. That was the main reason I didn't want to be a judge.

When I talked with the Navajo chief judge, we talked about many things, about many changes that have come about in today's world on the reservation itself and how the white man's society has now come to be a part of our reservation life.

Were you appointed? I submitted a résumé after the chief judge convinced me. They were telling me that there were several who had put résumés in for that position. All the judges' positions are two-year terms. We have to be reappointed. Well, they actually ask if you want to continue in the position and if you do, they usually just let you. Judges don't have to run for office. The Tribal Council are the ones who review the applications and they are the ones who make the selection.

I have been a judge about three months now. I'm fairly new but because I worked with the drug court program for seven years, I know pretty much the law and the procedures. I work with the criminal, the civil, and the children's court and the arraignments. We helped out with the tribal court if they need our help.

Tell me about the problems on the reservation. The main problems are alcohol and drugs. Meth has hit our reservation like wildfire in the past two years. Our criminal cases have skyrocketed because when these folks use meth it brings out a rage in them. There's a lot of domestic violence. That was part of what I discussed with the Navajo chief judge. Another part is parents not taking care of their own children. We have a lot of nonsupport cases because it goes back again to alcohol and drugs. They will work until maybe the first paycheck and then they are buying alcohol and drugs. That has really impacted our young adults. We don't see too many juveniles in court.

Does the school take any role in trying to help the children stay away from drugs and alcohol? Yes. They have counselors there and if the children are caught with marijuana at school or alcohol, they try to sanction them and handle it there at the school. But if fights break out at school then law enforcement has to be called in and the juveniles are then taken to detention. We have juvenile court and adult court. I hear both. I am the Children's Court judge. The chief judge has appointed me. I do criminal hearings and the children's hearings. The acting chief judge does all the civil hearings, she does the arraignments. She handles those cases and I handle the others. Of course, when she's absent I hear civil cases and when I'm absent she'll hear the children's or criminal cases. We back each other up.

I'd like to get to the basic question of whether you think the government and the white society are still killing Apaches. Will you discuss that? In my opinion, the use of meth comes from the neighboring towns of Albuquerque, El Paso, Alamogordo, Roswell. There are drug dealers from there who come to the reservation. Maybe they met a tribal member in one of the bars in the neighboring towns and befriended them. Later on had them try meth, got them on it, and then talked them into selling it. So they come on the reservation and bring the meth to tribal members and they become dealers. So we have actually had several cases come before us where homes have been raided by the BIA police officers and the tribal investigator, FBI people, and brought before the court where meth was found—just huge amounts. Only one time a home was busted where they were cooking meth.

Is meth the major drug problem? It is now. More than alcohol now in our young adults, ages eighteen to thirty. They get hooked on meth and then when they come through the crash they use alcohol and marijuana to help them through the hangover. So then they are hooked on alcohol and marijuana. It's three drugs then.

Is meth and its consequences one of the government's and white society's weapons that is killing Apaches? Oh sure. Yes. *How can you blame white society for meth use? The individual is choosing to use it.* It was white society that introduced the meth to that Native American. If that individual never did that, the Native American would never know about meth. Way back in years past, way back when my great-grandfather Naiche was still living, the white man and the Mexican introduced them to alcohol. There was no alcoholism. There was no cirrhosis of the liver. There was no tuberculosis, no diabetes. There wasn't any of that or the diseases that alcohol brought on. The same thing with marijuana—the diseases that come from that. Emphysema. That stuff is loaded with nicotine. One pack of cigarettes is equal to one joint when it comes to that.

Why did the government and the white society introduce these harmful drugs and alcohol to the Native American? I think that back when my great-grandfather Naiche and my great-great-grandfather Cochise were living, it was because they wanted the land. "There's gold here and we want it." Gold didn't mean anything to the Indian people. We lived with the land. The white people wanted the gold, the silver, they put up fences and they claimed the land. So, the Indian would ask, "Who did you pay to own that land?" Ussen[3] doesn't take money or any kind of payment for the land. They just took it. So they got the Indians drunk and killed their families off, like what they did to Geronimo when he went to Mexico with his warriors. While he was there to trade, the Mexicans invaded his camp, killed his wife and children, his mother, and many of the other elders and children who were there at the camp.

How does that relate to the use of drugs and alcohol today? I think because of historical trauma.[4] Because that happened back then, it's been carried from generation to generation to generation. I grew up in a home where my mom and dad drank, so I believed it was OK for me to do it.

Today, on the way to school the children have soda pop bottles in their backpacks that are filled with alcohol. They drink it at lunchtime or between classes. The teachers wonder why the children aren't learning. I think its historical trauma from the generations. They think that's the norm for Indian life. The only way you can be happy is when you're high. Or high on meth. Or high on some illegal drug.

Why would today's white society introduce meth on the reservation? Money. They want more money, more power. Maybe they will get to the point where the treaties that we signed will break and the government will take the land, the water. We will end up paying for our water, paying taxes on our land. *What else can they take?* Our language, our identity. The drugs could lead to all this and probably just killing off the Indians.

So the drugs are a vehicle to get from the Apaches over time what they want, the same as alcohol was in historical times? Yes. The white men are very sly, very sneaky. By introducing the Apaches to meth, we are killing ourselves. We get hooked on it. We have to have it. So right now on our reservation, our tribe has more young people enrolled than older people. When I look at that as a counselor, I see children starting to use drugs at the age of seven or eight years old. They are drinking alcohol because, like I said, it's the norm. The parents are letting them do it, or maybe the parents are passed out. Then Mom and Dad didn't finish that joint over there, so the kids spark it up. Also, there's some meth over there that maybe a twelve- or thirteen-year-old observed Mom and Dad and learned how to do it, so they're using it.

The way I look at it is when an individual starts that young, their childhood ends and they are in middle age. Their middle age ends when they are about eighteen and then they become an adult through their twenties and then become old. They are dead by thirty or thirty-five years old. That is how I see the lifespan of an Apache person on this reservation. We do have elders, we do, who were able to pull themselves out of that. Not all the elders went that way. There are a few of them who are—gosh—maybe 2 or 3 percent of the population, very small, that have maintained sobriety to get to their seventies. My mother is seventy-eight years old. She battled alcohol when she was young. She was able to pull herself up and I really, truly believe in my heart that it happened because my grandfather had to get stern with her. We had already lost one of my aunts to cirrhosis and then we lost my uncle to cirrhosis. Then we lost my grandfather to old age. My mom had one sister left and she died from pneumonia. My aunt Althea and my uncle Preston fell into that trap of alcoholism and couldn't pull themselves out.

You are saying that there is not much difference between the comparison you made of the historical times and today. Not much difference. *You believe there is a continuum from the very first exposure of the Apache people to alcohol because of an ulterior motive on the white man's part to today.* Yes. That same situation has existed for hundreds of years. I would say the main drug of choice today is meth. Meth is far more deadly. Meth can kill a person in two or three years whereas alcohol would kill an Apache, say, over a span of fifteen to twenty years when they end up with cirrhosis. With meth, it destroys the brain cells and the organs in the body a lot quicker than the alcohol does. That's why I think we lose a lot of our young folks to suicide because they go crazy, they go nuts. They can no longer comprehend life and so they take their own lives.

Is the suicide rate higher for reservation residents than those in neighboring towns? It is. It is a lot higher. We have had adults committing suicide along with juveniles. The way they do it is to hang themselves. There was one individual, a young man who hung himself in his closet with his shoestrings. Another one a week later and another one a week later. Almost every week there was a young person hanging themselves in their closet with their shoestrings. Copycat, I believe, is what it was. And then we had some young adults in their twenties following suit. Every single one of these individuals who committed suicide was alcohol addicted or addicted to a drug.

With all that in mind, what is the future of the tribe? It's obvious that drugs are destroying people and families, but what about your culture? Your language, your songs? Oh my goodness. Well, I think one of the positive things that has happened—and my mother was a big part of this—is that an Apache dictionary was devised. It started with my mother, Evelyn Breuninger, and Scott Rushforth. Scott is an anthropologist/linguist and works at New Mexico State University in Las Cruces. My mother was the manager at the Mescalero Apache Cultural Center and Museum at that time. She, Evelyn, and Scott got together and developed an Apache alphabet that is different from the American alphabet because there are sounds that we make in our language that they don't use in theirs. From that they translated the Webster's Dictionary into the Apache language and they translated a medical dictionary into the Apache language. Because of that the Apache language has been implemented in Head Start, kindergarten, and all the way up to twelfth grade in our school. It's taught in the classroom to the children. We were losing our language and we were losing our culture and traditions. I saw that when I was young. There was so much alcoholism and drinking. Feast time was party time. It wasn't a coming of age for the young girl. It was time to drink, have fun, and get drunk. Now I see a change in that. Even though meth is now the drug of choice, our children and grandchildren can speak the Apache language because it is taught to them in school.

I went to boarding school, I don't speak the language. Every summer when I came back my grandfather would only speak to me in Apache so I understand it fully and I speak some, not all. I can't pronounce some of the words. When I was growing up, with my father being Anglo, English was spoken in the home, English was spoken at school. During the summers I stayed with my grandfather. That's how I picked up the Apache language. So now it's in the school and the history of the Mescalero Apaches, the history of the Chiricahua Apaches, and the history of the Lipan Apaches are taught to our children. They learn about all three bands. Some children have all three bloodlines, some have two. Some—maybe their parent is Anglo or Mexican or we even have some tribal affiliates who are Negro. All the children are learning the language. They go home and speak it at home. That's one of the positive things that has happened. But, then when the kids get to the middle-school age, I think that's where they start experimenting with alcohol and drugs and they start losing the language again. Many drop out from high school.

Teenage pregnancies are just as bad as the meth here. Babies having babies. I know a ten-year-old girl who had a child. And then the following year had another one. She became a mother at a very, very young age. So, she doesn't go to school. She doesn't work. That has happened to many of our young girls. *Is that the white society's influence?* It is, because of TV. What they see on TV. MTV. All these things that the kids do on TV, they mock.

I was part of an interview project that we did with the kids in school back in 1995 and we talked to them about the language, the tradition, the alcohol. We gave them cameras and said, "Film anything you want." They interviewed some of the adults and asked, "If we didn't have a bar here on the reservation, what would you do?" Almost every single answer was, "We'd go to the neighboring town and get it." The kids then asked, "If you didn't have a vehicle, how would you go?" The answers were, "I'll walk. I'll hitchhike." A lot of those kids back then are now young adults and parents and some have fallen into the trap of alcohol and drugs. Back then they swore up and down that it wouldn't happen to them, but it did.

Please discuss the future of the tribe. Fifty years from now there will still be the coming of age ceremonies. I have seen an increase in interest in the coming of age ceremony during the past five years. One year we will have maybe thirty girls having their ceremony spread from spring through fall. Before, there were only eight or nine. The interest is increasing. That's hopeful. Yes. I see young men in the big tipi singing with their fathers, with their uncles, so they are being mentored and taught by experience, being right in there, singing with them, and learning the songs. These aren't taught in school, so the only way a child or an individual can learn it is by actually going and being a part of it. I also see that with the Crown dancers. The clowns are very young, little bitty guys, and they are starting out now to work their way up to be the first [Crown] dancer. You have to earn your position as you move up in the line. To become the first dancer is the greatest honor. So there's the hope.

Is it possible that the white man will own this land? It might be a possibility in fifty years. But, in fifty years I think the reservation will still be a reservation and I think the culture and tradition will still be there. As long as the language continues to be taught, I don't think we'll lose it totally. One of the things that I think is good, too, is that there is a gentleman by the name of Joseph Geronimo[5] who went to Eastern New Mexico University in Ruidoso and talked with some folks there. I don't know who all was involved with him but he got it to where anyone that is taking a college course and has to learn a second language, the Apache language can now be one where they earn college credit. That's also a positive thing. I think if more of our young folks take advantage of that, the language won't get lost.

In general, what do you see happening to the tribe? I would tease my dad and say we made an Indian out of him. I see in the future that they will make the Indian into the white man. I think the only way that an Apache is going to advance in this world in the future is to master the white man's ways and become like him. *Do you mean losing your cultural identity?* The lines I'm thinking about is that they are doing that to benefit themselves money-wise. To be successful an Apache must become a white man. They must take the white man's tools and become the computer experts, become the bankers, become the lawyers, and become a part of that white society. *How can they become like a white person and still stay Apache?* They can stay Apache. In their hearts they will stay Apache. Inside they will always stay Apache. But on the outside they will be forced to use those tools to be successful. If not, they will probably just be alcoholics and drug addicts.

How would you fix all the problems? What I would like to see, starting with the young children, is teaching them all the bad stuff that alcohol and drugs lead to. Somewhere you have to break the historical trauma being passed down generation to generation. We, us, the Apaches, we have got to break that. I feel that the only way it can be done is to start with our young people. Teach them the right way now. Teach them that it's not OK to drink. Teach them that it's not OK to party when it's feast time. Feast time isn't party time. Feast time is blessing time, prayer time, healing time. This is the holiest time. Teach them the importance of that and let them grasp it when they are young so they won't fall. If they experiment with alcohol, they will already know the negative part of it. "I tried that and I don't like it. I'll go on with my education." I would like to see people who care and who have compassion help do this in the schools. Our teachers are white teachers and there are those who work from the heart and there are those who work from the pocket. Meaning they are there just for the money. So, if we can start with the young, I think we have a chance of making a very good comeback, and the future I see is the Apache lawyers, the doctors, and the teachers filling the positions here on the reservation. Maybe even a governor, a senator, maybe even one day a president. A Native American can accomplish that but it has to begin with the young and it has to start now.

Is it being done? Right now the alcohol and drugs have a grasp on the part of the population of the tribe that can't pull themselves out. What is going to have to happen is that somebody else is going to have to take over in training their young, their children. We have programs to help them and they maintain their sobriety while they are in that program for that period of time. Many of them relapse, right back to where they were, but some of them don't.

Are these U.S. government programs or tribal programs? The drug court program that we have is funded through a grant from the federal government. We have an inpatient, outpatient rehabilitation center that is funded through government monies. It's true that there is never enough money from the U.S. government to help our people. We have to fight for every cent we can get to help.

We haven't talked about the health field. We are down to where our hospital now, if you are an inpatient, you're there to die. Your life is coming to an end because the doctors say, "There is nothing more we can do for you." When I talk to the doctors, I myself have asked the doctor, "Why was not more done for this individual?" And he said, "Because there is no money." I have been to the dental department in our hospital and asked, "You used to do root canals. Now all you do is pull the teeth. Why?" And he answered, "They don't have enough money to pay me to do the root canals. And they told me I can't do that anymore. So now my only option is to tell you that I can pull that tooth or you can go off the reservation and pay another dentist to do that root canal." People don't have the money. So we have a lot of Indians smiling with no teeth. Actually, a person's livelihood and health a lot of times is your teeth. Like everybody else, we have to chew our food for our stomach to digest and it really does affect our health.

Who is telling the dentists not to do root canals? The CEO at the hospital says, "Washington has cut our budget." Why? Because there's a war going on. The money needs to go over there. So, we are at the bottom. *Was it this bad before the Iraq war?* No. Our hospital used to deliver babies. They don't anymore. We had a doctor doing appendectomies. They don't do that anymore. They would take care of you in a second. *This has all changed since the war?* Yes. We used to have a twenty-four-hour hospital. Now they are open from eight in the morning until ten at night. If you have an emergency after ten o'clock until eight o'clock the next morning, you have to go to a neighboring town's ER and that bill is on you. That's why a lot of Indian people lose their lives. If they are having chest pain and they know the hospital is not going to pay for a major surgery, or something like that, I know many who will stay home and suffer. It has changed since this war. There is no money. Our health care has gone down since the war. Yes. But, even before the war the federal government was cutting monies to our IHS facility.

Some of the people we visited with talked about the hospital as conducting experiments with drugs. For example, if someone appears with chest and left arm pain and nitroglycerine should be the drug of choice, they might give the patient something else for high blood pressure because they don't have nitroglycerine. Have you heard about anything like that? I have heard many, many times that we are just guinea pigs. That's what the tribal members say about our hospital. They will try different medications on us and all of a sudden we see on TV that the USDA, or whoever is in control of the medicines, says the medicine they gave us is now being banned because it causes this or that.

And those medicines are being dispensed on the reservation? We have had those medicines on the reservation. And I have seen where it seems like they even want to see how much pain the Apache can tolerate, so they will give you a dosage of a pain medication that is low. They are kind of monitoring to see how many can tolerate it. Then they have to raise it for another group. Even with antibiotics. To me, I feel that when there is an antibiotic that comes out, we are the ones they are going to try it on. How many people react to it and what kind of reaction is there.

Those studies have to be ordered. In other words, someone on the reservation doesn't decide they are going to do that. Do you have any idea where that would come from? I know the main office to our hospital is in Albuquerque. So, I assume it comes from there and they get it from the federal government. *But you believe and you have determined that you are being used as a study group?* Oh yes. Another thing we see is that the interns who come make many, many mistakes. Our people are diagnosed wrong because they have interns there that use us to learn. If I'm becoming a doctor and I go into this hospital and I am diagnosing these people while I am there to find out if I'm right. I'm learning by trial and error. If you should die, then I'm sorry and I'm not going to let it happen to the next ones, maybe.

Who supervises these interns? Is there a doctor in charge? There's supposed to be an MD on duty with the interns. Not now. *There are interns functioning as doctors in charge, learning on the Apaches?* Yes. And these are only temporary. Some are here for thirty days, some for three months, some you can't understand what they tell you because their accent is from the other side of the world. We have a doctor here now from Haiti. Our clinical director is from Brazil. They have these real heavy accents and they talk real fast. Sometimes I have to slow them down so I can understand them. Now I go in there and the doctor says, "You self-diagnosed and you are right." Then I'll tell him what medications I want and he says, "OK." He puts it down and he gives me what I want. I already know what's wrong with me and I know what medications are going to fix that. I'm not going to let him give me penicillin when I know the other antibiotic Cephlex will work. Then people are allergic to medications.

Are there many people on the reservation who have the medical knowledge that you do? They don't. In working with the drug court, there's many times I have heard of tribal members in our program who have different illnesses being diagnosed wrong and given the wrong medication. They will even tell the doctor they are allergic to the medication and yet he still gives it to them. "It makes my heart go ninety miles an hour and he still gave it to me," they will say.

Why would a doctor do that? I don't want to say that they take advantage of the patient, but maybe because the patient doesn't know. I think the medications that are prescribed should be explained more because I have been in there with my daughter where the doctor says, "I'm going to give you this medication that will help you from throwing up, and I'm going to give you this medication for the earache, and I'm going to give you this medication to help you with the pain," and he never says the name of it. You go out there and are waiting for your medication and they call you and give it to you. When we get home, I will read it and say, "What is this they gave you?" "This is for my ear." Well, it's not right. I opened the bottle of medicine that was supposed to be an antibiotic and it was Tylenol 3, a pain killer. I took that bottle of medicine back to the pharmacist myself and told him, "Look, this is not what it is supposed to be."

So there is a pharmacist on the reservation. Yes, at the IHS hospital. There are people in there who are not trained, who don't know what the medications are. Or they are just learning and they don't have a licensed pharmacist while the one that is in training is giving the wrong medication. My mother got wrong medication that made her deathly sick one time. I went back to the hospital and told them that my mother is allergic to many drugs. They will look at the doctor's name on the bottle and say, "Oh, that doctor left last week. He's not here anymore." So it's the doctor's fault. Things like that happen. Today it has gotten even worse. I don't think any of those doctors at the hospital are American citizens. I think they are doctors from abroad and they are here learning. America seems to be the number one country and is a lot of things in a lot of people's eyes. But we American people know better, especially the Native Americans.

Now the hospital is the place where you go to die. Now when someone is admitted to the hospital there's a lot of vehicles up there. One of my co-workers lives right next door to the hospital, so when someone is really sick she will tell me. The next day or so that individual is gone, has passed on. They say, "There is nothing more we can do." They are there just suffering and dying in that bed.

Is there any area that we should have discussed but didn't? I would also like to comment on our housing situation on the reservation. There are two or sometimes three families living in one house, eleven or twelve people. We need more housing. We have homeless people here too.

Also, I think within the past two years one of the improvements I see as a plus for our people is the art program. There was an art program implemented in the Empowerment Building and it is managed by one of our tribal council members. Because of that they have art shows at the Inn of the Mountain Gods, which is one of our major tribal enterprises where only our tribal members are allowed to sell their artwork. I have seen a lot of them take advantage of that. In the past they had the artistic ability to carve or paint and they never used it because they drank all the time. Now that program will provide them with the paint and canvas, everything they need to start them off. They eventually have to pick it up themselves because they will start selling their artwork.

Is that funded through a government grant? I don't know but I am assuming so. I think that's a good thing that was implemented along with the Apache language classes that they have now too. I see hope in that.

Is there a lot of artistic ability in the tribe? Oh, yes. There's so much out there that, if given the opportunity, they would take advantage. But a lot of them have no money. A lot of them don't have a job. There aren't a whole lot of jobs on the reservation. I think a lot of our people have fallen into the trap of alcohol and drugs and don't use their artistic abilities to improve their lives.

Also, non-Indians are put in the manager positions and supervisor positions, so our tribal members are under these people and are treated with bias and end up losing their jobs. No one likes to be disrespected, and they are.

But, I do believe Ussen will change things for the better and I have faith in our culture and traditions to make things better for all. I thank God for putting me here in this beautiful place—Mescalero, New Mexico—and I'm proud that I am a Chiricahua Apache and a direct descendant of Chief Cochise.

—September 18, 2008

TESTIMONY OF LARRY SHAY

Good afternoon, I'm Larry Shay. I am a longtime member of the Mescalero Apache Tribe and I carry the title today as the War Chief for the tribe. I have been a Tribal Council member for nineteen years, appointed in 1986. I missed a couple of turns for a couple of years, and I have been fortunate enough to serve nineteen years.

I was born in 1951 here in Mescalero, Elk Silver district. Born out in the country and was transported to the IHS for evaluation. I have lived lifelong here in Mescalero among my people on the Mescalero Apache Reservation. My previous name was Larry Pebeashay. My father is a Comanche from Oklahoma, Harold Pebeashay. My mother is Mescalero and Lipan Apache. I never knew my dad, really. I probably was three or four years old when he left and I grew up fatherless until I was probably 12 or thirteen. I had a stepfather. But anyway, I was fortunate enough to have grown up in Mescalero with the Mescalero Apache influence along with maybe a little of Lipan Apache influence. I think I'm going to continue to live here until I'm called home, whenever that may be. To tell you the truth, I am really fortunate to be Apache among the Mescalero Apache people. If I was asked to live my life all over again, I think I would choose the same, Mescalero Apache in Mescalero. That's how proud I am and how fortunate I am to be who I am.

When I first was aware of myself, realizing that I was a living person, I was probably three years old. I'm almost certain that when I started my life, the communication between my father and mother was probably English. My father didn't speak Apache, my mother didn't speak Comanche. After my father left I was immersed in the Apache ways of life, the culture, the language with my uncles, my relatives, the elders. As I said, I have lived lifelong here in Mescalero and I grew up Mescalero Apache. That's who I am. I am more aware of my Mescalero Apache ancestry than I am of the Comanche and the Lipan. The Lipan people of Mexico, New Mexico, Texas, and Oklahoma, as I was told, were a subgroup of the Apaches that lived somewhere in Mexico and the Gulf of Mexico. *Where are you connected to them?* Through my grandfather's side. His Christian name was Pedro Mendez but I don't know his Indian name or the name he was going by before Pedro Mendez was given to him. The way they got their Hispanic or Spanish names was because of some of the contacts they had with the Spanish and Mexican people. My grandfather, I believe, came to Mescalero in 1902, somewhere around there when the Lipans came to Mescalero. My grandfather, Pedro Mendez, and another brother, Julio Mendez, came with some other people from Mexico. *Are there any Lipans still on the reservation?* Yes, but most are mixed blood with Mescalero and Chiricahua here at Mescalero. The last full-blood Lipan I was told was Pasquala Venego, a grandaunt of mine.

I went to elementary school here at Mescalero, from first grade to second grade. Third grade, I went to boarding school at the Santa Fe Indian School and was put back into second grade. I remember going to that school and that was the time when my eyes were opened to the wider society, or the dominant society. I lived and went to school at the boarding school for that one year, around 1956. It opened my eyes to the other ethnic groups of people—Hispanic and the like. It didn't shock me by any means but it sort of just gelled with me in the sense that it didn't surprise me but I became somewhat aware that there were other people besides the Apache people.

Do you remember anything significant that happened during that year in the boarding school that stayed with you? I wasn't aware of why there were boarding schools. All I knew and understood was that it was a school and that I went there to learn. And I didn't know the government's scheme of indoctrinating the Indian people. I didn't know those behind-the-scene concepts. When I was in the Santa Fe Indian School I was comfortable. I had three squares, a warm place to live, and clean blankets and was taking a shower every day. The school had electricity. We had television sets—black and white. Those were some of the things that were advanced at the time—the early 1960s.

For a summer break, I came back to Mescalero and I remember wanting to go back but I guess I was not told I was needed at home for financial purposes. I wanted to go back to boarding school but my mother wouldn't let me probably for the fact that she was getting assistance. If I were to stay around, the state assistance would include me in the family assistance. So, I was held back from going back to boarding school. Unfortunately, those are some of the years that I lost some educational progress.

Did you want to go back to get the education? To get the education and for nutritional purposes and to be away from the unpleasant circumstances of life. Alcoholism was great problem with a lot of parents. I didn't want to be a part of that situation but I was made to be. It could have been an escape for me and I probably would have done a whole lot better than I did regarding my education.

Did you finish grade school? I finished grade school in Mescalero and went on to Tularosa public school and things didn't change really well for people in my generation in the '50s because of the influences from the wider society in regard to alcohol and other things that hampered life on the reservation.

Do you see that same situation here? To a degree, yes, we are still experiencing that and that's probably one of the reasons that hampers our efforts in regard to safeguarding our language and our cultural knowledge. There's a whole gamut of things that really hamper our efforts to regain our Apache culture and way of life. The Apache language and the culture and the ways are somewhat put on the back burner and at present I see that people don't have the time to really practice the language, culture, and tradition mainly because of jobs and keeping up with the Joneses and making a living. Money oriented.

Do you have military service, or did you leave the reservation? The only time I left the reservation was to attend boarding school. Like I said, I did go to the Santa Fe Indian School as a preschooler. I found out for myself that I was probably better off at the boarding school trying to get an education instead of some of the predicaments of staying home at Mescalero with alcoholism and other factors. But I did go back to boarding school as a sophomore at the Albuquerque Indian School and then back to Santa Fe as a junior and senior. And I finished school in '71. I stayed in Santa Fe for another five years as a postgraduate and along with that I was working for the late artist Allan Houser for another three years. I got a fine arts degree in two mediums—drawing and painting—and in three dimensions—sculpture. And the other was photography. I took some classes in linguistics and I have some credits from the University of New Mexico from the staff who came to the Institute of American Indian Arts in Santa Fe. They were giving credits in regard to writing your native language whether it be

Navajo, Pueblo, Sioux, Cherokee, or Apache. They helped with some of the disciplines. I guess it was linguistics, phonetics, etc.

How have you made your living? First through fine arts—drawing, sculpting, and painting. I have done a lot of things. At one time I was a maintenance man, I was a Park Service man, I was even a conservation officer and I was a construction worker. Also, I was a surveyor with the Bureau of Indian Affairs and worked with the natural resources of the tribe, the Natural Resources Department of the BIA, and I worked at the hotel facility—the Inn of the Mountain Gods. Through the arts I worked with the Mescalero Apache School in the departmental area of gifted and talented students for two years. We are presently in the year 2008. About three years ago Joseph Geronimo and I proposed a program to the tribe called the Cultural Enrichment Program. When we brainstormed to make that a reality we discussed the concept or the idea that the tribe needed support for their traditional and cultural aspects. We agreed that it would be a good idea to have a program to teach the language, the tradition, the culture, and along with that the arts, whether it be crafts or fine arts. The tribal leadership under the Sara Misquez administration and Butch Blazer's education subcommittee for the Tribal Council gave us a blessing to start the program. To this day we still have a workshop for fine arts and Joseph Geronimo has the program for the language and traditional culture classes. We have the old school facility which is now the Cultural Empowerment Complex just next to the Community Center at Mescalero.

Do you do any artwork now? I am an artist at heart. I hardly practice it. I'm a support person and I long to go back to my production in the arts but there's just not time. To do so, in my job-related position as a Tribal Council member, might be a conflict of interest, but I do support and help the local artisans.

Is your tribal position paid? The council position is an elected position and has been so since it started, I suppose. The only paid positions for the government body are the president and vice president. They are full time. The rest of the members of the council only get paid stipends when they are going to attend a meeting, do business for the tribe, and discuss the maintenance of the tribe.

What are the major problems on the reservation today? Oh, there are a whole lot of problems I see. At times I wish I had a magic wand to correct everything, but that's impossible so we just have to find ways and means of trying to address things as they come, not to say that we are neglecting other things of equal importance. The number one thing that bothers me is—I hope I'm not a hundred percent sure of this and I hope I'm not correct in assuming—that the language will be gone and that the cultural traditions will be gone. It concerns me. I think that we are somewhat fading in regard to our Indian-ness as Apache people. I hope I am not correct in this assumption. I'm just wary of losing it and it concerns me the most.

Do you see the language and culture fading away? To a degree, yes, with our youth. There's a small segment of our youth that are somewhat attempting to maintain our Apache-ness but there's just not enough time in the day and not enough resources to really get a handle on it. To a small degree some of our youth are making an effort to learn the language, but it takes more than that. To be an Apache you have to have grown up with the language, the tradition, and culture. You must have been saturated with the Apache way of life. It takes an Apache person to really understand and appreciate it. For myself, I think a lot of our youth have missed that opportunity because of the wider society's influence. I was probably fortunate when I first came into the world and heard the Apache language spoken. I heard the language being spoken when I took my first breath. It's not so now. In the mid-'70s, English was the first language newborn Apaches heard.

What are some of the problems that the dominant society has put onto the people here? Mainly, I think it's the isolation of the reservation boundaries. They have somewhat established us to have a small piece of land. What I'm saying is that it hampered a lot of things, like the way of life of the Apache people. We were nomadic. We were free to do as we pleased and not be restricted. We could have gone to Mexico, to be together, to be carefree from being somewhat policed or restricted from practicing our language and traditions. The reservation might have its good intentions but then again it might have its negative impacts and restrictions. *Versus the prior nomadic lifestyle?* Yes. So, it's kind of like an oppression. You get isolated and are restricting somebody from other things.

Are there any problems that the dominant society is placing on the Apache people currently? Yes, I think so, in many forms. The Apache people were not dependent on this lifestyle as they were before. It's kind of like conditioning a person to be dominated, conditioning them so that in a sense the only survival is an eight-hour job, and influences like electricity, transportation, all these modern things. It's not to say that this is bad, but in a sense it is, and has had a negative effect on the way the Apache people had gotten along with their own language, customs, and traditions, even [the way of] thinking of the Apache people. That all has taken a back seat.

I listen to the elders praying. When prayers are spoken in the Apache language, it impacts differently on your mind and your soul. *Can you give me an example?* The Apache people around here all address the Great Spirit and the importance of being spiritual and having a solid understanding of respect and thankfulness and gratitude to all the life-giving sources that the Creator has given the Apache people. The air, the water, the wildlife, the medicines and many things that the Apache people don't take for granted or dominate the resources. Take what you need but not much more than what you need. My perspective is that we all are comfortable-oriented, and convenience-oriented in 2008. We want things now—lights, electricity, fast transportation. Those conveniences. If you are aware of your traditions, and you have experienced being without conveniences, the traditions have a way of teaching that there's poverty, and there's also abundance. It will be really detrimental if you've never experienced poverty.

So you see the influence of the dominant society as harmful, detrimental to the traditional Apache way—the fast food, fast cars, electricity. Those are some realities in 2008 for myself, yes, because those conveniences are irreversible. You can't just ignore them. They are there.

I'm aware that we at Mescalero have a lot of shortcomings, deficiencies, and lack the resources and the money to really address our concerns in regard to our cultural language and the like. *Does that mean you are going to be absorbed by the dominant society as you fight to retain your traditional heritage?* I'm reluctant to say that's going to happen. I hope it doesn't happen. I'm really crossing my fingers. But who am I? I am not a fortune teller. But I just hope that here at Mescalero we give some effort to try to address our situation, in regard to saving our traditions, language, and our culture. It's going to be a big order, a big task. If we don't take on the task, who will? That's the bottom line.

As to the future of the tribe in fifty years, what do you see? I see two things fifty years from now. First of all, I'm frightened to look down that far and predict. I think that the way we are going now, the conversational Apache language will be limited. Hopefully it will survive.

Is it just going to fade into the future or can you put a time and date on it? In Mescalero—I'm going to do a little bit of guessing here in regard to the spoken Apache language. The Lipan language is still spoken by a fairly few people. My mother speaks it and she's seventy-seven years old. The Chiricahua language has a little more people speaking it than the Lipan language. And the dominant language now is Mescalero. From 5,000 people, maybe 1,500—I'm guessing now—speak it. And the Chiricahua language, a little less than that. The majority is Mescalero. The Lipan language is almost out of the picture. Probably 1 percent, maybe a bit more. But in fifty years from now, out of 100 percent, maybe 50 percent will still speak the Mescalero language. The Chiricahua language will probably still be around but the Lipan language, I'm almost certain will diminish even more.

Do you have hope for the future? For the tribe? Yes, I have my hopes for the tribe. I noticed that in the schools the language is being taught and it surprises me. Some of the kids can count up into the hundreds which to this day, as for myself, I can only count to five. But I'm fluent in the Apache language. I never really practiced the numbers. Some of the kids who are ten, twelve, thirteen can count into the hundreds. But the conversational Apache, oh boy. If it's going to survive, the tribe needs to get really aggressive. If they really want to save the language they need to do some drastic things.

How about the ceremonies? Are they going to fade or are they going to remain? The ceremonies are religious in nature and are still practiced so they may continue, but I am concerned about prayer itself in the Apache language. When I hear an elder praying, I can almost feel the words of the prayers. I can almost identify with the prayer itself. I can almost wrap it around me, be comfortable with it, and understand the prayer. But in about twenty years from now, that shroud of understanding prayers will have a lot of holes. It's not going to be as meaningful.

It will still be here, but the understanding won't? Yes. You can almost see a circle with holes? And people won't understand. Yes. *That's a beautiful way of saying it.* That's what I mean. But of course I could be wrong in twenty years. I'm hopeful that I'm proven wrong.

Do you think the reservation, the land, will be here for the people? Oh, that's a tough one. I'm going to say this. The government has broken a lot of treaties and promises and I don't think the people will give up the little boundaries they have left. They're not going to give that up without a fight. There will be challenges because the wider society—the state and the U.S. government—are looking at the resources that belong to us: the land, the water. And that's going to be an issue, the hot topic and controversy in the future. There's going to be a lot of attempts for control and to take over the reservation. But I don't think the Mescaleros will let that happen. Hopefully we will have some people fight back just to keep the reservation. Our main survival is the land we have to practice our own way of life. To have our own government. To have our own say-so here in Mescalero.

Are you saying that if the government takes the land away, the tribe won't survive? I'm almost certain that's going to happen. Once the dominant society takes over, we're just going to be absorbed. *And they can take the land?* I heard that by the stroke of a pen they could.

Do you really see that happening, Larry? Boy, that's a tough one. I don't see it happening without a fight. But, if it should happen, there's going to be a fight. I don't want to say it's not going to happen, or it's going to happen. I'm at a loss but I hopefully wish that it doesn't happen. There has to be something that can be done in regard to settling once and for all without opening a can of worms.

Of all the questions that we have asked you, is there anything we should have asked? I would just like to say that we are in a time that started maybe back in the '50s where we are being somewhat conditioned by the dominant society's way of life, the conveniences. I'm concerned about the language, the culture, and the traditions, and I would like to, before ten or twenty years, see the tribe really make the best effort possible to address or to put something in place to save the language, the traditions, and the culture. No matter what amount of money it's going to take. No matter what sacrifices have to be made. We have to do it. We have to do that! It needs to be done and that's that. It needs to be addressed. Nothing else will do.

—June 11, 2008

Conversations

THE HORSEHOLDERS

TESTIMONY OF ELIZA YUZOS

I am Eliza Yuzos, I'm twenty-nine years old and I live with the Mescalero Apache Tribe. I am an Apache, half Chiricahua Apache, half Jicarilla Apache. I don't work, I stay home with my kids. I'm known as a "home-maker." I have four children who are ten, nine, eight, and four. *Were you born on the reservation?* Yes. *Have you ever lived off the reservation?* Yes. When I was about thirteen I lived in Roswell, New Mexico, for a while. I lived in Dulce, New Mexico, for a while.[1] I lived in Washington for a while. My mother was Valerie Muniz. She was from Dulce and my father was Danny Richard Kanseah Sr., from Mescalero. My mother was Jicarilla Apache and my father was Chiricahua Apache. I went to school here in Mescalero, in Dulce, and Roswell. I didn't graduate. I dropped out when I was in the eleventh grade because I was pregnant at the time and had a lot of issues going on in school and at home with my Mom. The school didn't give me any help so I had to drop out. They didn't really accept the fact that the girls were going to school pregnant. It was like they were looking down on you because you were making a bad impression on all the other young girls. Every day at school I always had problems with other teen-age kids, plus the principal. I had to take off school to go to the prenatal doctor's appointment. They were getting mad when I missed school and I just got tired of it. This was ten years ago. Actually, today it is a lot better.

I was going to school with my little girl when I was twenty-seven years old; she was only two. While I was in school for half a day, she was in school and I was taking my GED classes upstairs. But now they don't have that program anymore. They just had it for two years. They had a lot of kids going there but they weren't making progress. The kids weren't graduating; they weren't trying to finish their GED so they just closed that program down. *Did you get your GED?* No, I just quit going back and then my little girl got sick when I was working. She got pneumonia.

Do you like living here on the reservation? The housing area where I live is not much but it's nice. I have a house of my own, a government house with four bedrooms, two bathrooms, and two showers, and it fits me and my family just right. *How did you get this house?* We all lived there together—me and my brother, my sister, and my Mom. After my Mom moved out, my brother moved and he and my sister went their own ways, and my brother gave the house to me. *That's what you like about the reservation?* Yes, that I have my own house and I pay my rent—$25.00 a month—utilities, and my bills myself. I get money from the state for myself.

What don't you like on the reservation? It's hard to get to the hospital when you need it. I wish they had a van that would come and get you and take you to the primary care doctor. *You don't have your own transportation?* No. *So, if you have a sick child in the middle of the night . . .* All you can do is just call the ambulance from Ruidoso. It takes you to the hospital in Ruidoso. *Do they respond quickly?* No, they usually take their time, but they do show up. I usually don't go to the Ruidoso hospital because to me they are not nice to Indians over there. They are real prejudiced. When my little girl was sick with pneumonia, they were so rude to us. They wouldn't attend to her. She sat out in the lobby forever. She couldn't breathe. *And how is it at IHS hospital here?* They treat you pretty good. If you have an emergency like that they'll see you right away. *In the middle of the night, would somebody respond from the hospital here on the reservation?* They will just send out the fire and rescue people and then wait for the ambulance to come from Ruidoso.

Will you talk about the social problems on the reservation—the drugs and the alcohol? Yes, it's real bad here. Every way you turn around there's alcohol and drugs. Meth is real bad. I think meth is taking over Mescalero. *In your age group?* Yes. *At what age do people start using meth?* Probably eighteen on up to late thirties. *What can be done about that?* If they could find the people supplying the reservation . . . *Who is supplying?* Mexicans. *And they are bringing it on to the reservation?* Yes. *Should the government do something about that? After all, this is a federal reservation.* I really don't know. They might have undercover agents, but they need to get into the supply chain and find their way. A lot of these younger people give them trouble and the only way they will narc out somebody is so they won't have to go to jail. That's what I see a lot of.

Other problems? For example, single mothers? Yes. A lot of the parents would rather drink and not take care of the kids and the kids hang around with their friends because they are the only ones there and then they start doing bad things. It's just constant. *Are you saying that the parents are drinking and so the young people have no one to turn to?* Yes. *Are the parents also taking drugs?* Probably some, yes. Mainly the younger people. The older people prefer the alcohol. *Does the government help in any way?* I think they just throw their hands up and walk away. They don't want to put anything on the reservation for people to get help or anything like that. *Are they ignoring what's happening here on the reservation?* They just walk away. *Why?* There are a lot of people who want to quit drugs and alcohol but they have no where to go to have somebody support them or a support group or anything around here like that. *Is there anything the tribe could be doing?* Yes. The tribe could be getting programs together to help the alcohol and drug people.

We have been talking with many people about the health care at the hospital. You think it's good for your children. Is that right? Not really, because it's hard to get them on Medicaid and it's hard to keep them on Medicaid. If your kids are sick they don't try to get them out to a hospital where they can get help. They just give them medication that will help them out for a while and that's it. My daughter has a real rare skin problem and nobody knows anything about it. They just say it's eczema. It's not eczema, it's something else. She needs to see a specialist but they won't do anything to help her. *Are you talking about the hospital on the reservation?* Yes. And they always have different doctors there. You can never see the same doctor again. And the only reason I keep taking my kids back there is if I take them off the reservation I don't have the money to pay for them to get seen.

How can health care for your children be improved? Medicine-wise and transportation to go see a doctor, better medications. *If you take your child to the Ruidoso hospital and the doctor gives you a prescription for an antibiotic that the reservation doesn't have in its formulary, what happens?* Nothing. I will have to take it back to Ruidoso and see where I can fill it. If I don't have the money there's nothing I can do. The Mescalero hospital won't help me. *Would they offer to give you another drug?* They'll say they have a substitute for it but then they rarely do that. They say, "Oh, we don't have it," or "We can't fill it." *By "substitute" do you mean another medicine or a generic?* A generic. *To your knowledge, do they ever change the prescription? Let's say it's for antibiotic* A *and they don't have it. Would they give you antibiotic* B *instead?* Yes, probably. *If the prescription is not generic, would they give you another kind of drug?* No. *Would you have to go back to Ruidoso to fill it, or not fill it at all?* Yes.

Would you go to a medicine man for help? No. If my child is really sick, I don't think they can help. I know they can help by telling me what tea is good and things like that but they won't help them in a way that they need medicine. *Even if you're desperate and don't have the money to fill a prescription, you would not go to a medicine man?* Yes.

Suppose your child was bleeding, what would you do? Does the hospital have any type of emergency care? Yes. You have to sit a while and wait at the hospital even though the kid is gushing out blood, fifteen or twenty minutes at the most, but if they are real sick you have to wait like everybody else. You have to sit. When my daughter was sick with pneumonia, I had to sit almost a whole hour to get her seen. Then when I got her seen and got her in there, her oxygen was so low, they rushed her to the Ruidoso hospital. She was so dehydrated that they couldn't get an IV started on her. She had a relapse last year. She was in Las Cruces in the hospital for pneumonia again. This is my baby, the four-year-old one.

Who pays the bill? Oh. I had to take the bill to the Mescalero hospital but then I got a bill saying that I had to pay for it. They sent it to me and I took it to the Mescalero hospital and they said they would take care of it. Then I got another paper saying that they didn't have the funds to pay for it. *The Mescalero hospital did not have the funds?* Yes. Then I had to start paying money to that bill. *Or what happens?* They keep sending me letters for payment. *Are they satisfied with $15 or $20 a month?* Yes. *How do you feel about that?* It gets me cranky because they say they'll take care of it, send them so far to get treated, and I still have to pay for it. And I don't have the money to pay for it.[2]

How would you change it? Have more doctors there, have more caseworkers to help you with your child and your bills. If they say they're going to take care of it, then they should take care of it instead of sending it back to you and saying you have to pay this much. And they should tell us that at the beginning that public health doesn't have the money before they send them all to a hospital. They should say we have to pay for it.

Let's talk about something else. Do you speak or understand the traditional language? I understand some of it but I don't speak it. *Did you have a puberty ceremony?* No I didn't. I was supposed to have one with my sister but I ended up pregnant. *Do you know the songs?* Yes. I hear them and I know them. *Do you think the sixteen- and seventeen-year-olds know the songs and the language?* I would say that some of them do and some of them don't. There's a lot of them that hardly even understand the traditional songs. *Are there girls that go through the puberty ceremony who don't know the old language?* Yes. *If someone doesn't understand the language, how can that person know what the medicine man is saying?* I have no idea.

It sounds as if you believe the tribe is losing its culture. Yes. Some of the younger generation doesn't understand or they don't know it. *Who is at fault? Do you blame anyone? Anything?* No. Growing up, my mom always used to talk to us but I just can't speak it. Now my kids talk to me in Indian and I understand it. They know songs in Indian from the school, and I'm glad. They sing "Jingle Bells" in Apache and they know how to count up to sixty in Apache. They know all their animals in Apache. I am proud of them. They know more than me. They learn different things in their Apache class than we did when we were going to school. Now they have papers that they bring home. Coloring papers with Indian ladies. At the bottom of the paper is the word "brown" in Apache to color her skirt. They have all sorts of neat stuff like that. It's more than we ever had when I was in school. I don't know what they do in the high school because my kids are still in the lower grades. In the Christmas program they had at the school my daughter sang an Apache song and my other daughter sang the "Twelve Days of Christmas." She does it different. She sang "five turquoise rings, four Indian feathers, three Indian blankets, twelve Indian baskets." My son Damian has a drum in his room and he sits with his buddies and they sing because they sing at school. He's ten years old. *So your children are teaching you.* Practically. They are. What I don't know, they tell me.

We understand that there have been many reductions in funding reservation programs. Do you think it has anything to do with the Iraq war? To me, it seems that everything got more expensive. Before, I used to go to the store with $100.00 and I could buy a lot of groceries with that. Now, it won't even cover what I'm going to cook for that night. *Do you get food stamps?* The kids get it, but it's not much. They only get $200.00 in the middle of the month.

Given all the problems, what does the future hold for the tribe? I don't think we're going to have a tribe. There's just going to be open land for the white people. I don't think we're going to have a tribe. *What does that mean to you, to your children, and to your grandchildren?* We should be happy with what we have now for what we have here on the reservation—the open land—because in the future we might not have it. *Do you think the government will take the land back?* Yes. *And then, what will happen to all the people here?* We probably will still have our little community houses here and there but a lot of people from the outside will be moving in.

What does it mean to you to be an Apache? I'm very proud to be an Apache. It's my language, it's my heritage. It goes way back. Customs. I hope it lasts. I believe it will. My kids are proud to be Apache. The tribe, the language, the songs will never be lost.

You have hope in the future of the Apache identity, but you're not sure about the future of the reservation land. If you could make certain that the land, the people, the identity lasts throughout time into the future, how would you do it? I would want the land to stay the same and the language to be spoken fluently. I wish we could go around talking like the Mexicans but in our language. I have three girls and I would want them to have something that I never had—the puberty ceremony. And they are already looking forward to it and they aren't even ten years old yet. I tell them, "You better slow down." I don't want them to become teenagers. Being a teen on the reservation is hard.

Does the puberty ceremony make a difference? Right after having the ceremony, the girls lose their virginity. They right away pop out kids. They right away do what they were told not to do. *Do you think the ceremony has anything to do with it?* No, it's just the way I see it. There's nothing on the reservation for the teenagers to do. That's why a lot of them drink and drop out of school and end up being moms early. I wish there would be a program for teenagers to go to just hang out or teach them new things instead of having them run around here and there.

Has the government ever asked the people what they want? No. *Would you like it if the government came on the reservation and sat down with the younger people?* Yes, that would be nice. That way they could find some way to help the community, a place where they could go instead of running around here and there. It would be a place where kids and teenagers could go and call their own—just for the young kids.

Is there anything you would like to add? I would like to see the language get going more, get the drugs and alcohol off the reservation. The border isn't that far away and that's why everything comes up this way.

—January 10, 2008

TESTIMONY OF DAN KANSEAH JR.

My name is Danny Richard Kanseah Jr. I'm thirty years old and I have lived here at Mescalero on the reservation all my life. My great-grandfather was Jasper Kanseah, Geronimo's youngest warrior who was thirteen years old when they surrendered in 1886. I am employed at Ski Apache—the ski resort we have here on the reservation and that we own and operate. I have been up there going on eight years. I enjoy my job a lot. I am a year-round employee working away from everything, away from all the turmoil down here. In the winter I work in the ski rental shop. In the summer I work at the golf course and with building maintenance, painting buildings, and repainting towers on the ski trail. I have made a lot of friends from everywhere.

Is Ski Apache under Apache management? Management runs through from the Inn of the Mountain Gods.[1] The majority of management is mainly Anglo people. They are training a lot of Apache people. The last I knew was an MIT class—Manager in Training. They are giving Apaches a lot of opportunities to jump in there and see what they want to do, if they want to move up any higher. It's the second year they started doing this and quite a few have jumped in there. Things are changing around up there a lot. There's a lot more people from the reservation getting involved, trying to become up in higher places, want to do things like as manager-type, trying to move up in there.

Do you see that trend of more Apaches involved in other places on the reservation? They started off when they redid the Inn and they moved the ski area off the old Inn. The white people were all in the higher places. Now with all the classes and training they are starting, a lot more people are getting involved. Well, it slowly started. It slowly made its way. They got new management, it went under the Inn, a lot more people spoke out. They have open meetings with us at the Inn and they tell us straight out, "Do you have any problems with your managers, with your supervisors?" The Tribal Council sits there and listens to everybody. Anybody who wants to say things will stand up, say what they have on their mind, what they don't like, what they want done, certain things that they see that they want. All I can say right now is that it's growing a lot more with the Apaches getting involved, now that they are starting to open up and let them do trainings. They are sending them places. It's all through the tribe.

Please explain what you called "turmoil." I tried working for the Forestry before and that's a government job. The way I see it going is that you either have to know somebody in high places or most of your family has to be working up there before you can get in there. I lived up there, right below the forestry, for years and I've seen it happen so many times. *You are saying that it's not what you know, it's who you know with a government job.* Pretty much. I see it quite a bit in a lot of places here. *In government agencies on the reservation?* Basically down here and all over the place. *With the tribe too?* It's either that or it depends on whether they really want to get into office, they are really into it. That's most of the way I see it.

What are the problems on the reservation for young people of your age? One thing would be the alcohol. That's one of the main deals here that's real bad. Alcohol and drugs. The meth got real bad here. Probably for about four years it's gotten real bad. I've been around to see different things happen and I've seen the way things change from people smoking pot a lot. Now a lot of it is meth. It's real bad. You see people change. You see the way they used to look and now. I've read about it, seen videos about it. It's scary.

Does the tribe or the government offer programs to try to help these people? Are they good programs? Do they work? As far as I know, they have rehab here but other than that, every time you talk about getting sent somewhere, anything like that, it's always that they don't have any money, they don't have any help. *The tribe or the government?* They say the tribe but I don't know if rehab is through the hospital, the government. I'm pretty sure it would be through the government but everybody says the tribe.

How can the alcoholism and drug problems on the reservation be fixed? The way I see it is teach them while they're young. *Education.* Yes. I grew up—pretty much we lived all over the state and moved from here to there—on my own, started working young. At times I went out and did things that I regret now. I think about it now and I'm trying to change my life. I talk to my nephews and my nieces, even some of my younger friends and I tell them it's not worth it.

Where should this type of education begin? In the home? In the schools? In the churches? I feel it should be everywhere the kids go. It should be in the church, pretty strong in the schools. People say it always starts at home, though. It's real bad here. You see it everywhere.

If the government recognized this problem and were to come here on the reservation with a program to discourage drugs, would young people attend that program or would the court have to intervene and demand that they participate in that program? That's really hard to say. There's some that are strong, there are some that are willing to get out of here, try to do something. A lot of them just think it was in my family all my life, my mom, my dad did it. They just think, "That's the way I'm going to be." That's what I see a lot of around here. *So a government program would not help?* It all depends on if the person really wants it. There are a lot of people around here who could do real good without the drugs and alcohol. *Must it be court ordered, part of probation, to force them into it?* That's the way most of them will quit. Either they get a term in jail—if you do it next time, you're going to go longer. It takes somebody to really get hurt, even to pass away, and then most people start thinking about it. It's a sad way to turn yourself around but that's the way I see things go around here.

Who do you blame for the persistence and extent of the use of drugs and alcohol? The individual? The government's lack of involvement on this federal reservation? The outside society's impact? The way I have grown up and done things that I regret now, it's really fifty-fifty. It's not anybody's fault and it's everybody's fault. It's all mixed into one. My mom used to tell me, "They didn't make you drink it. You don't have to." There are very few people who will do it, don't like it, and they won't ever go back. That's the way I feel about it. You can either stop it but there are very few people who will try it once or so and they won't like it. And then there are people who can't go without it.

Is there a government educational program on the reservation to deal with alcohol and drug addiction? No, everything is court ordered. Right now the only place I know of is the rehab they have here under the tribe. *It's tribal sponsored?* As far as I know, it's tribal human services. Other than trying to send you somewhere, they always say, "We don't have any money." The tribe doesn't have the money. They always say "the tribe," never "the government."

Besides help for addictions, what do people need that they are not getting? There's a lot of broken homes, one-parent families. Either the father or mother is stuck with the kids and there's a lot of domestic violence. It all turns around to the alcohol. That's how I see it. I've been to jail and when people come in I see them and talk to them and ask why they're in here. "My wife or my husband turned me in because I got in a fight with them." And then it all goes down to "he said or she said." They blame each other. When you ask them what they were doing, they say, "We went out to so and so's party." That's the way I see a lot of things around here.

How about the health care for young people? I've been to the hospital quite a bit for different treatments. It takes a long time to get in there, for one thing. You sign in and you'll sit there for who knows how long. I guess it's fair in health care but I feel they could do a lot better. *How?* Doctor-wise, for one. You go down there and there's one doctor. You go maybe the next week, it might be somebody else. You get used to one doctor that you've had for your family for so many years. And all of a sudden they up and leave and somebody else comes in. *How does it make you feel when all of a sudden there's a new face?* I've done it before and kind of felt weird because you go for certain things. I had a head shunt and they removed it and I had problems with my back. Through my whole file there was a doctor I had for a while that knew what was going on. Then they leave and it kind of frustrates you because you go back in there and they have to thumb through everything and figure out what's going on all over again. That's why I'm glad that I have my own insurance through my work now so I go off the reservation if I need anything. The thing is too—it's like the hospital here is like a store. It's open whenever. Sometimes you have to be there by a certain time or you won't get seen. Weekends, as far as I know, it's not open. I've called down there and nobody answers the phone. They always tell us that we have to go to Ruidoso. I've been there on weekends when I catch a cold. They may be open until noon on Saturdays. After that, they close the doors. I think it's not even open on Sundays.

Is the emergency room closed or is the hospital closed? The whole thing. If you have an emergency, everything comes from Ruidoso. The ambulance comes from Ruidoso. I was seen in Ruidoso before I had my insurance. They told us to give the bill to the IHS here in Mescalero and they will either pay it or help you with it. A lot of times I have been turned down. They say, "We don't have the money." *And so they come after you?* Yes. That's why now I have my own insurance through my work.

It's always been this way. The closing of the hospital—I really don't know when that started. It's been a while since I've been there. Now I don't even bother with the hospital. *So you are discouraged.* I see things with my grandmother. She used to go down there for her diabetic clinic. It's like the same thing every day. It's like you take your car to a certain place for an oil change. You know what they're going to do every time. It's the same thing they do down there. You need your medicine. There's a lot of things they could be doing for the elderly but I don't see it.

Let's talk about education. What do you see as a cause for a young person dropping out of high school? Why wouldn't a young person remain in high school? A lot of what I see around here goes back to what I said about broken homes. They don't have support. A lot of the young people turn to alcohol and drugs. The drug and meth got bad around here. It usually starts around the high school age. Teenagers. *You don't see it in elementary schools?* No, not that I've known. I go over there a lot with my sister for her kids. They teach them a lot. I've learned a lot with the younger kids. They're starting to show them. With the older ones, I've seen that from broken families they have no support. Their parents are off somewhere drinking or just not home. It's rarely that you will see someone finish and go off to school. College or so. I haven't seen that in a while. There's some who drop out but very few go back. Most of them just give up. Don't bother with it. *What becomes of them?* A lot of them start working. Since I have been at the ski area I have seen a lot of young people going up there. I look at some of them and wonder why they aren't in school.

Is it because they want to stay on the reservation, they're afraid to go off, or they just don't see the benefits of an education? I feel a lot of them are afraid to leave. It's like the reservation and the life here is what they will always know. I've seen a few go off to school but for some reason they always end up coming back here. *With an education to do something positive here or coming back because of having given up?* I've seen a lot them just come back and then I've seen some of them go off for a semester to two and come back. Then you see them start working. I had a couple of friends who went off to military service and they came right back and are still here. They just work. There's some, too, who start partying.

Is it a fear of white society and failure out there? Being from here and being native—some of them come back to their families and they think that's the life they're going to live. *You are talking about giving up.* Yes, pretty much. It's like, "I don't think I'm going to make it out there. It's easy here." They are in an area where they feel like they are safe and they can do pretty much anything here. It's easy to get a job. But once you start, you are at the bottom. It takes a while to work your way up. Plus you don't have an education. That's hard on them too. They do offer programs for some of the kids who drop out. They offer GED classes and computer classes and different things. I had a couple of friends who went off to the service, came back, and started working.

How much of a role does discrimination play? Around here, a lot. In Ruidoso it comes down to the Indian people who hang around town and drink a lot. They make names for themselves and then others who go into town shopping get looked at a certain way. They think, "I know what they're here for." It's like that with a job. "Well why are you trying to get hired here? You don't have an education." I talked to some friends who have come home from school and tell them they should keep going.

How about military service? Is there a lot of appeal for young people to join the military? Do the recruiters come here on the reservation? As far as I know, the school has a Career Day. I see them over there. But other than that, I don't see them come on their own. *Do the young people sign up?* Only very few.

How would you fix the dropout problem? The truancy?[2] They do a lot of teaching traditional ways at the school right now, but it would also have to do with getting parents involved so the youngsters can see that their parents are behind them. So they can talk to them about it, helping them, being there for the program. *The parents would have to be willing.* Yes. There's a lot of kids here who don't know how to talk to their parents. They are scared. All they know is that everybody else is doing it. That's what I see around here.

The future of the tribe? I feel the music, the songs, the traditions, the culture slowly fading away. They offer programs to learn the language and it's ignored. *Do you speak your ancestral language? Understand it?* No. I can understand it pretty much. I just don't speak it. *Do you know anybody of your age, your friends, who speak your grandmother's language?* Two. They're not fluent. They can talk somewhat. I feel that it's fading away. *Did they learn it at home or at school?* At home and in the school. Right now there could be a chance for the kids now—my nephews small as they are. They're showing them now to learn Apache and they come home and talk to their mom. But what I see in a lot of them is that they are real shy about it. They're open in class. I watched my nephews, went to the school. They're real open around kids their age and the teacher but when they get out, they grew up with English. It's hard for them to practice it. *Why?* With the younger kids, their parents don't even know it. I guess it's kind of hard for them to go home and try to share it with their parents because some of the parents don't know it themselves.

If the tribe is fading away, will it be replaced by something? There will be very few who still understand and know what the original religion is. There will be blending with everybody else and just go mainstream. *Do you think you'll be living on the reservation?* I feel it will still be there but everyone will just fade out. I feel that the Mescalero Apache Tribe will be on a reservation and a tribe but the language and all that the elderly know is the main thing that's fading out. There's a lot of people that don't get involved anymore. It's hard to teach somebody something. There's some who grew up not going to the "doings." The parents are not interested in it anymore.

The puberty ceremony is one of the hallmarks of being Apache. How many in your age group come to the puberty ceremony and appreciate it for it's religious meaning? Now what I see for the younger generation is its something to party. Something just to get together with your friends. You don't really see them out there getting involved with the singers or the dancers. *Someone recently commented that after the puberty ceremony the girls think they are ready to have babies.* There is a lot of really young parents around here. I feel that's why a lot of them dropped out and don't go to school because they're going to have kids. It's around here quite a bit. Most of the ones that do understand the ceremony, I guess they respect it and respect what it's all about. As I was saying, it's slowly going. The tradition and everything. Back when I was small, there were tons of feasts. One was going on over here, another over there. Now it's like maybe one or two a month. I see it slowly going.

Are you a role model for the children in your family? I pretty much started with my sisters' kids. As I said, I've done a lot of things in my life that I regret and I think about it. I look at them and think that I'm their only uncle and I have to try to be there.

—December 6, 2007

TESTIMONY OF KIANA MANGAS

Hello Kiana. Please spell your name for us. K-i-a-n-a M-a-n-g-a-s. I'm sixteen years old; just turned sixteen. I live in Mescalero, New Mexico. I had lived with my mom in Oklahoma but we moved back. *With your dad too? His name is Carl?* Yes. *Do you have friends?* I have only one friend, my best friend, Brandy Little. *Do you have plans for the future?* Not really. I think the future will come to me when the right time comes. *Are you thinking about going on to school after you graduate?* I'm thinking about going to a culinary arts school or art school. Now I'm in tenth grade here at Mescalero.

What's the best thing about school? Math and art. *Is there anything you don't like about school?* Not really. But I'd say my Apache class is the only one I have a problem with. It's called "Apache 2" because my teacher told us that in Apache 2 you learn about the tribe and what the tribe does for the people. But all we have been doing this whole time is reading a book. *What is the title of the book you are reading? Indeh.*[1] There are some parts of the book that I don't really "get." *Did you have "Apache 1"?* Yes, in my freshman year. We learned our language there and how to use words and converse. When I was in middle school, my teacher worked real good with the students and our language. I knew some of my words from then. Since I have been in high school all we do is recap what we did every year. I am not getting used to it because we don't speak our Apache language in class.

What is difficult about Indeh? They tell different sides of the story of what happened to the Chiricahua before we were imprisoned, from Daklugie's side to Eugene Chihuahua.[2] Whenever Daklugie talks about what happens, he keeps going to flashbacks.

How do the other kids accept the class on Apaches? Do they want to learn more? The teachers tell us that our language is dying and we are the only chance we have. What I think a lot is that if our language is dying, why don't they teach us our Apache language instead of talking to us in English? Why can't we have all Apache teachers who talk to us in Apache? In every class. *Have you voiced that to the school?* I told that to the counselors at the school. They just write it down in a notebook and forget about it.

Do you have special activities at school? I used to play volleyball and basketball but I really don't play sports here anymore because I don't want to play for a team that's just going to keep losing. The coaches don't want to work with you. I belong in arts and culinary arts. I really like my arts class. My teacher is inspirational to me. She's from Ruidoso. *What is your specialty?* Whatever is in front of me I use it. How I get my inspiration is that I think about what happened from the beginning to my people.

From before the imprisonment when they were free? You think about that? Yes. And how we used to have our own land. Well, we had territory between the different groups of Apaches and Pueblos. We had our own large territory from the Chiricahua[3] mountains to Silver City, New Mexico, and into Mexico toward Chihuahua. Whenever we went to the rock near Tres Castillo in Mexico, where we used to pray to Ussen, he would tell us something or would give us a way by talking to us. Whenever I think about animals, birds, bugs, that's how I do my art.

Can you tell us about your family's history? I come from the generation of Mangas Coloradas,[4] and Victorio[5] and Lozen.[6] My great-grandmother is the late Evelyn Gaines and my grandmother is Claudine Saenz. We were prisoners of war until my great-grandmother came here from Fort Sill. When she came here she started her life. She was born in Fort Sill but they brought her here when she was a baby. I helped take care of her.

Did she pass anything on to you? Teach you the old ways? Or does your grandmother do that? My grandmother Claudine tells me stories and my godparents also. *Who are they?* Karen and Harlyn Geronimo.

Talking about your Apache history and tradition, do you wish the school offered you more? Yes, like having a teacher who would want to work with the students instead of making us do something out of a book. Like read instead of talking our Apache language. I don't like it when teachers judge you. How they judge you is what you look like, how you act. *Are these Apache teachers?* Some of the teachers at our school . . . We have five teachers who are females. They are Apaches from Mescalero. Then we have only one male teacher who works with the kids. He's the Apache teacher for the middle school. They sometimes only pick people they want to work with. They are assistant teachers. Like when homeroom teachers are not there, that's when the co-ed teachers come in. *But you have an Apache teacher teaching you Apache history with Eve Ball's book, correct?* Yes. *Is that the only book you are using?* Yes. *Do you wish there was another book that gives another side of it?* Yes.

Are there any issues at school with drugs? Oh, there's a lot of issues with drugs. At our school they caught students drug trafficking during school. Selling. Just marijuana. Whenever we moved in up here, there was a man who lived down the road from us who used to have a meth house. When they built our new neighborhood on the reservation. About a year later we started noticing there was a lot of cars that used to drive by real fast during the night. It's not really a problem where we live anymore because they told the man that he had to leave. He is banned from the tribe. He can't come back.

Are there a lot of kids involved at the school? Just two boys who are always getting in trouble for that. I would say it's a major problem in some parts of Mescalero and probably a major problem at school. *Even though only two kids are dealing that you know about? Selling to other kids at school?* Yes. *When does it start?* Probably mostly eighth grade and up. *What's your opinion of taking drugs?* I think that the people who are doing this should just grow up and get a job. It's not hard making money. You just have to put labor into it. They don't want to do their own thing, like get a job and keep a job. They would rather sell drugs.

How about the other problems? Teenage pregnancies, for example. When I was in middle school, one of my former friends was pregnant when she was in eighth grade. She was fourteen years old. That's the youngest I have ever known at the Mescalero School to get pregnant. She had her baby and she got her baby taken away from her because she couldn't take care of him. Now she goes to school when she feels like it. She acts like she's the main part of school but she hardly goes to school.

Do you see that as her problem, or is the school not doing enough? Are her parents not doing enough? When we started school, the school told us that we have only five absences that we can take if we are sick. If we have any more than five absences, then they are going to take it to the court and find out what the issue is about why we have so many absences. But I think that since the school never enforced that rule that the students are just going to do what they do. Not go to school.

Do you see teenage pregnancies as a major problem or just that one person you know? That person, and when I got into high school, my ninth grade former friend got pregnant too. This was near the end of school and beginning of summer. She dropped out of school and said she was going to try to get her GED so she could become a nurse over here at the Care Center. I told her to finish school, that it was better for her instead of getting a GED. A GED is just like a lot of tests and it would be hard for her. Why not do something easier for herself?

Do you think there is a lot of sexual activity going on among the students? I think so. They just don't get caught. *What about the young fathers in all this? What role do they take?* My friend who got pregnant when she was in high school, her boyfriend is going into the army to help support her and the baby. *Do the young fathers stay around a lot or are they absent?* It just probably depends on how they connect with each other, talk. If they always fight and fight, he's just going to leave her and say, "You're just one of my points." *Points?* Whenever guys get with someone and have kids and they don't take care of them.

Do you see any of this in your high school environment? Not this year. *Overall, drugs, sex, or any other issue. Do you see it as a problem or do you see it just as a few people having those problems?* I would say a few people.

Let's talk a little bit about your puberty ceremony. How old were you when you had your ceremony? I was thirteen years old. When I turned thirteen I told my grandmother that I wanted to have my feast. *Why did you want it?* I wanted to make my parents proud. *Did you?* Yes. *What is the attitude of the other girls in high school about having the ceremony? Why do they choose not to have it?* If there's a girl who doesn't want to have her feast, it's the girl's choice or the mother's choice. *Why wouldn't they?* They just want to be naughty all the time. They don't want to grow up to be a mature person. *So you see the puberty ceremony as helping you grow up in the right way?* When you prepare for the ceremony, you do it all yourself. Your medicine lady—they call her your mother because she's there taking care of you—helps you gather all the stuff but you have to prepare it yourself. She helps you gather the soap for when they bathe you and the singing sticks and the sticks that go around the fire on the last night.

How long does it take you to prepare? We started in the winter of 2005 by getting our stuff. After I turned thirteen we started getting our stuff. After I hired them, they gave me a week, and then we went out to gather our stuff. Your medicine lady teaches you what to do. She tells you what is going to go on.

Whose dress did you have? Your grandmother's? My grandmother Claudine made my dress for me. My dress is yellow and blue is the main color. On the top it has mountains. *Did you choose that symbol?* No. Like they say in the old ways, it will come to you. Like, when you start with the buckskin, it will just come up. It's like a story. Once you start, it will finish itself.

And then the ceremony is held and that's a very exciting time. What happens afterward? Did it change you? I gave myself a year before I started changing, because you're still a child for a while. When you take off your buckskins they tell you you're grown up but you still feel like you're a child. So you give yourself time to bloom.

Then you were fourteen. Did you feel yourself changing? Not until I got into this year. Sixteen. I feel I've grown up. I've learned a lot from the ceremony. *Now that you are sixteen, can you look back and see the benefits of having the ceremony. Compare it how you think you would be if you didn't have it.* I think if I didn't have my ceremony that I would probably act the same but be like how all these other girls who didn't have their ceremony. Be running around all the time. Getting into trouble. Since I had my feast, I know right from wrong. It strengthened me to be good.

Was there a special feeling that it gave you? When the first day came I was nervous. They tell every girl on the first day to not be nervous, just stay calm, it's like a normal day, but this is your special day. You're going to become White Painted Woman in a couple of days. When you put on your buckskins you still feel the same but with a little bit more weight on you and you just have to pull yourself through that way. They call you White Painted Woman, a healer. When you have your buckskins on, you are a healer. Whoever comes to you, if they ask you for a blessing, you cannot say no. You have to do it. That's what my godmother told me. She's the one who told me how to heal their spirit. Make them feel better.

That must have been quite a thrill for you. Can you still feel it? Yes. White Painted Woman will always be with me, just like Ussen is with us. She was the—how do I say it?—giver of life to us with her sons. Her sons then gave us life. They brought us here. As a people.

The girls who don't go through the ceremony—do they support you still or do they give you a hard time about it? Well, I wouldn't know because my best friend had her feast too. We're always together. *And you don't associate with many other girls?* No, not really. Just us.

What about the role of boys in your life? None. *Is that deliberate? Do you choose not to have any?* I chose one but it was a mistake.

Your goals now. Art school or culinary school? Do you want to go to school and then come back to the reservation? I told my mom that when I turn eighteen and finish school, I'm going to go my way. I don't know what this is yet, until Ussen tells me. I think I can do it on my own. *Ussen might bring you back or He might take you somewhere else.* He might bring me here again or he might take me away. It's OK, wherever She takes me.

If you had all the money in the world, all the resources and could change what you see on the reservation that is not good, what would you change? I would change how our affiliates above us make their decisions. *You mean the Tribal Council?* Yes, and what we expect from them for being in council. Like we chose them to make choices for the tribe. I would like to let them know that we are still here. *Do you think that they are overlooking the people in their decisions?* No. I would change it to make—like how the Inn of the Mountain Gods is—they don't hire Indians hardly ever from here and they shut down the sawmill and the fish hatchery. I would fix the sawmill and the Inn—having people mostly from here working at the Inn. Because that's a tribal industry. If we don't have hardly any tribal members there, how can we let them know that we're still here?

What would you say to the council as a teenager? What do you do for activity? We had a workforce for teens—working over the summer. That's what I did last year. But this year they're not having it. Only for adults. Last summer I worked for the Carrizo Boys and Girls Club, going toward the Inn of the Mountain Gods. I worked with the little children and I really enjoyed it. They won't have it for the teens this year. You have to go through the school.

When you hang out with your friend, what do you do? All we do is just sit and laugh. That's our thing. We're kind of like clowns. I watch movies.

I like movies. I don't to read very much. I don't know if I'm going to do sports yet. I think the reservation should have more activities to work with the kids. Like Joseph Geronimo used to work with the kids in his Apache language classes here at the Empowerment Building. He used to encourage kids to go to his classes by paying them out of his own pocket. I don't really know if he still teaches. *Would young people attend those classes without getting paid to do it?* I think some would if they were really encouraged by their parents and peers.

The future of the tribe. You're sixteen and you're going to be around for a long time. Whether you're here or off reservation, you're still an Apache and you have a family history to be very proud of. What do you see happening to the tribe? Going down. Our people are getting bigger. The Apache population is getting higher on the reservation and the workers who represent us are going down. Just like how our economy is. It's going down. *Why is the Apache workforce going down?* Selfishness. They want everything. Many clock in and some leave and don't come back. They stay clocked in until their hours are done and they're not doing what they're supposed to be doing.

Do you see the puberty ceremony surviving? Yes. *Do you see your language, your culture, who you are as Apaches surviving?* Our Apache blood is still running. We're still here. Yes, I see it in the future. What we need here is people who want to work instead of just clock in, leave, and go home. I see the language surviving through the little kids, the kindergarten kids. They really know our language more than I do.

When you look at hope for the future of the tribe, what is that hope based on? I wouldn't really know how to say this, but our hope is based on learning. The little kids have only one Apache class, like us, every day. A language class. The kindergartners' teacher knows more Apache than my teacher. I think if they would concentrate more on the little kids than us, they would be able to bring back our language.

So you see hope for your tribe in the children? Yes. I know I'm still a child. *Do you see the puberty ceremony continuing, the songs and the traditions continuing?* Yes, whenever I ask someone in the seventh grade, someone who hasn't had their feast yet, if they are going to have it. Some say no. Some say they are still thinking, they don't know the answer yet. Or yes. Just to have it. Well, just to have it doesn't mean to have your feast and be naughty afterward. It means to understand how it goes, where it came from.

Are you saying to the others that they should have a feast? I try to encourage them. Whenever I go on trips with the school, when we sing to the elderly, I ask them to bring their buckskins. They tell me they don't have a buckskin. And then I think that something must have happened to them, that they must have done something very upsetting to not have a feast.

How much of this is financial? What would happen if a family doesn't have the money? My dad worked on the fires. He wasn't a firefighter but he worked with the Forestry here. They went everywhere to help with the wild fires. That's how we got most of our money. If a person can't afford it, they should go to the council and ask for help. *So it's not financial reasons why they aren't doing it, it's personal?* Yes.

Do the girls have their own reasons for not wanting a feast? Is it because it requires a commitment? It does, and some girls just don't want to do the work. They don't want to work for themselves. *In years past, the ceremony was very sacred. Now I see it becoming more social. What do you think about that?* I think that becoming more social is telling the BIA in Washington that we're still growing, we're still going to be here no matter what you throw at us. We're going to be here forever. *So you see the social aspect of it as being all right?* Yes. *Do you see the girls today as seeing the ceremony as very sacred?* The girls who are younger than me, they sometimes treat it like it's just a joke. I was told by my medicine lady that you treat your dress like it's a part of you. Some girls don't.

If a girl doesn't understand Apache, and only knows English, how does she know what's going on during the ceremony? When I had my feast I really didn't know that much Apache. All I knew was my numbers and days and birds. Whenever you go through it, your medicine people will talk to you in Apache. All you have to do is just listen. Whatever they tell you in Apache, they will ask if you know what it means. If you say no, they'll tell you in English what it means. They will teach you some Apache too.

Now for the future leadership of the tribe. Do you agree that the tribe has to change to come into the twenty-first century? Yes, I agree with some of that. I think the only thing that shouldn't change is us. Since we all know technology, we can bring some of it here but we do not correspond a lot with it. *Do you see a problem remaining Apache and still progressing alongside the white society?* No. We can still be Apache and still progress along. *Keep your traditions, keep your ceremonies, keep your identity?* Keep our language. Yes. *And still survive as a tribe in the twenty-first century?* Yes.

Why do you believe that? How I think we could do it is that we just have to push ourselves and learn all the things we knew back then so perfectly.

You say you see hope in the young children. Is part of your hope for the future of your tribe in Ussen who will take care and protect and love the tribe no matter what. Yes. Because in Eve Ball's book Daklugie said Ussen will always take care of us and will always be with us. We're part of him, our Creator, our Father, just as Jesus is with you. You have heaven with Jesus and we have our Happy Place with Ussen. Ussen will always take care of the Apache people. He promised the Apaches that we will have our land back. We don't know when officially it will happen but I trust that it will happen. I think about it all the time. I dream about it sometimes. *So your land will be restored like it was before the white man came.* Yes.

Do you go to any Christian church? I really don't go to church on Sunday. I just go to the Reformed Church here. My family is a member.

Do you see a conflict between the way you look at Ussen and the way the Christians worship Jesus? Not really. To me when Pastor Bob talks to us at the church, he tells us that there's nothing going to be different between the two. He said they're the same. He tries to talk about Ussen and Jesus and how God is there. He understands the Apache way and how everything for the Apache is together. I follow what he says because he talks about both God and Jesus and Ussen. But if I had my preference, I'd go with Ussen.

Is there anything else you would like to say? I would like to say that Ussen is with us and he will always be with us. He will be watching over the Apaches forever.

What does it mean to you to be an Apache? I would say to be a fighter, a person who will never give up until the end. *I think you are a spiritual person who can talk to the bugs and the butterflies and listen to what they say. Would you agree with that?* Yes. How I would agree is knowing that we didn't give up for what was ours to begin with. We fought for our land for so many years and they couldn't take us down, not even the smallest band of Apaches, thirty-five with Geronimo. He had Power. Medicine. Lozen too. She had Power. Knowing that we have medicine and we have our own Power—each Apache has their own—it just takes some time to get to the part where they realize what their power is. Some books and movies tell how their Power was astronomical. There was no end to it. But even the Apache scouts in the army couldn't find us in Mexico. When we would go to Mexico they still couldn't find us and that's when they started sending in thousands of troops. That was before all the Border Patrol and immigration came in. I am thinking of how hard we fought the Mexicans and the white people. It makes me feel a little stronger knowing that I have that in my blood.

—January 30, 2009

EPILOGUE

The Unyielding Fire of Hope

The Apaches whose words you have just read and whose faces you have now seen in photographs have given you a rare glimpse inside a culture that for hundreds of years has been portrayed and defined by others.[1] Perhaps some Apaches endeavored, in the distant past, to tell their story and were rejected, mocked, or prohibited from doing so. Or, perhaps they didn't trust anyone to accurately convey their concerns and so they didn't speak out. Or, perhaps they were reluctant because they were worried that anything they said would jeopardize their security in a nation long hostile to their existence. Regardless of the reasons, these contemporary Apaches have now slipped out of the past restrictions and prepared the ground for future generations to be heard.

These modern voices ebb and flow with worry, with anger, and with criticism as they truthfully present the current conditions of their tribe. To most, inadequate health care, addictions, dysfunction in all its disguises, tribal politics, and the federal government cause apprehension, if not alarm. Readers may conclude that most of the problems mirror those occurring in the larger surrounding society, and that is also my belief, but the white man is not in danger of losing a rich, irreplaceable history and culture.[2] Euro-Americans' ethnic backgrounds have already been compromised by the popular and proverbial "melting pot" from which everyone ideally emerges cloaked in cultural anonymity.

Not so the Apaches. Their words reveal a people and society still somewhat intact culturally but not yet recovered from five hundred years of continuing imperialism, still reeling under the smothering layers of colonialism and colonization, and still being punished by an oppressor using today's weapons launched from a toxic dominant culture. There is no rehabilitation on earth able to completely negate or even neutralize the effects of this violence.

Oddly, or possibly not, after all the conversations, all the descriptions of problems, all of the "fixes" mentioned, the one prevailing emotion that flowed across the generations from elders to warriors to horseholders was hope. Hope may seem to be an unnatural response, even somewhat unrealistic, given the tribe's current and historical experiences with governments' intentions and outsiders' exploitation. But take a closer look.

Hope in the hearts of ancestors on the Spanish and Mexican colonial frontiers kept the Chiricahua Apaches determined to overcome what they correctly interpreted as destruction of their culture and desecration of the land entrusted to them by Ussen.[3] Hundreds of years later, hope continued to live in the minds of the Chiricahua Apache descendants, imprisoned for nearly three decades by the United States.[4] After release from confinement and despite having witnessed the deaths of many friends and relatives from communicable diseases, hope was still alive and was rejuvenated in the freedom they had long awaited.

Hope allowed the Mescalero Apaches to endure the years at Bosque Redondo, years of starvation, years of being forced to live side by side with former adversaries.[5] Hope thrived when, in 1873, the government withdrew 720 square miles of land from public usage and, through the president's executive order, established the Mescalero Apache Reservation in south central New Mexico.

Hope bloomed in the lives of nineteen surviving Lipan Apaches after they were removed from their west Texas homelands and transferred to the Mescalero Apache Reservation in the early 1900s.[6] Safe now but greatly reduced in population, they were no longer targeted and hunted mercilessly by Mexican and American armies.

Today, these descendants guard and preserve the fire of hope that sustained their ancestors through long years and horrendous experiences at the hands of their enemies. Each of the speakers is living testimony to the everlasting Apache spirit, a quality that neither the guns of the past nor the modern weapons of the twenty-first century can silence. They will survive as a tribe and their rich legacy, especially the hope that has sustained them for centuries, will live on in the bones and blood of the future generations.

In the words of Kathleen Kanseah, "We're Apaches, and we will never give in, not as long as one drop of Apache blood flows in our veins."[7]

REFLECTIONS

This book was conceived in Oklahoma, born in Arizona, and came to life in New Mexico. It was back in October 2007 when Marian and I were respectfully wandering from grave to grave in the Apache prisoner of war cemetery at Fort Sill that the idea of this book was first spoken aloud. Between then and the last interview in January of 2009, a fifteen-month period, much had happened.

We put thousands of miles on Marian's car, driving a fourteen-hour round trip once, sometimes twice, a month from Arizona to interview and visit for at least one week with our friends. We spent thousands of dollars on lodging and food. When we backed out of my driveway for the trip to Mescalero we never knew what we'd find once we arrived, or even how long it would take us to get there; one or two trips lasted five and a half hours, most were seven hours. We still haven't been able to reconcile the time warp, especially since we followed the same routine each time.

The array of our experiences at Mescalero was sweeping: someone became a new grandparent, someone was fired, someone was hired, someone lost a loved one, someone had emergency abdominal surgery, someone purchased a new car, someone stopped smoking, someone fell in love, someone considered divorce, someone "got religion," someone found a kitten, someone had food poisoning, someone lost an election. And so on. We felt we had to be on our toes all the time or we'd miss out on one of the most enriching periods of our lives.

My previous books were about the history and culture of the Chiricahua Apaches and so I usually spent hours upon hours researching in university libraries, museums, church archives, online, and such. With the exception of *Women of the Apache Nation,* none of my other books was about living Apaches, so this was a brand new endeavor, especially since it also involved the Mescalero and Lipan Apaches, friends whose ancestral history was new to me. I quickly learned that although the groups were once distinctive from one another, that uniqueness had long vanished due to the closeness of reservation life. A blending had occurred over the years, so most of our interviewees carried the blood of all three; the pride in being an Apache spread across all the groups.

I deeply understand and appreciate that pride. I see it as a manifestation of ancestral survival, ages-old courage, and everlasting hope. I can envision today's speakers surrounded by the wreckage caused by their modern enemies, yet standing tall, faces uplifted, thanking Ussen for all their blessings. I look into the future and I picture today's children in tribal leadership positions and even as national officials in a country free of stereotypes and welcoming all contributions. And then I look backward and there are the ancestors, watching, praying, and silently guiding their descendants into a brighter future.

My gratitude to the speakers and Marian Kelley is limitless.

—H. Henrietta Stockel
Tularosa, New Mexico

NOTES

Preface

1. It is said that the late Mildred Imach Cleghorn, chairperson for many years of the Fort Sill Apache tribe, some time ago smashed a bottle of champagne against an Apache helicopter, thus "christening" it at the invitation of the American government. Is this true or just another chapter in the Apache legend?

Author's Note

1. Nearby, a spaceport is under construction, to be ready for space tourists as early as 2011, at a cost of $200,000 per traveler. *Time* magazine, December 14, 2009, 10.

2. One popular account attributes the name to J. Robert Oppenheimer, the scientific head of the Manhattan Project. Another source cites Robert W. Henderson, head of the Engineering Group in the Explosives Division of the Manhattan Project. For more information, see Trinity Atomic Web Site, at http://www.cddc.vt.edu/host/atomic/trinity/trinity1.html.

3. Kidwell, Noley, and Tinker, A *Native American Theology,* 185n13.

4. Hoijer, *Chiricahua and Mescalero Apache Texts.*

5. Opler, *An Apache Lifeway.*

6. Ball, *Indeh: An Apache Odyssey.*

Introduction

1. Traditional storytellers decided what would be told, what would remain hidden, and when it would be spoken. Tales could include descriptions of derring-do, adventures, landscapes, landmarks, unfamiliar flora and fauna, mysteries, sacred sites, people, witches, dreams, and past events and encounters. Most tales would include moral lessons or examples to be used as guidance through life. Storytelling preserves a tribe's past, provides examples and explanations that direct and shape an individual's code of behavior, and recalls a culture's history. The storyteller had the heavy responsibility to inspire another generation, to instill pride, and to revitalize whatever aspects of tribal history were in danger of fading into obscurity. Regardless of accuracy, which is highly prized, however, orality in general always presents and preserves significant aspects of a group's history, and so the importance of a storyteller cannot be overestimated.

2. Sister Juanita Little, interview with author, December 6, 2007.

3. For more information, see Stockel, *Salvation through Slavery.*

4. An inspiring slogan based on a core concept that "Americans are destined by divine providence to expand their national domain." (Lamar, *The New Encyclopedia of the American West,* 699).

5. The Lipan Apaches surrendered in West Texas and were consigned to the Mescalero Apache Reservation during the years 1906–09. Some Lipan Apaches believe it was 1903–05. Accounts differ.

6. Literature on the Bosque Redondo experience, particularly for Navajos, is extensive. Regarding the Mescalero Apaches, the most informative document I found is titled "The Story of Bosque Redondo," and is available at the Bosque Redondo Memorial, Fort Sumner State Monument, P.O. Box 356, Fort Sumner, N.Mex. 88119, (505) 355–2537, at www.nmmonuments.org.

7. The Mescalero Apache Reservation was created in 1873 by President Ulysses S. Grant's Executive Order for the Mescalero Apaches who had been confined to nearby Fort Stanton, New Mexico.

Speakers

1. Ball, *Indeh.* This book is a classic.

2. For more information about the events on the Spanish colonial frontier, see Stockel, *Salvation through Slavery.*

3. The Warm Springs people comprise one of the Apache bands classified under the umbrella term, "Chiricahua." One of their most famous leaders was Victorio. His sister, Lozen, was the most famous female warrior in Apache history.

4. Stockel, *Women of the Apache Nation,* 88–99.

5. One of the most brilliant war leaders about whom several books have been written. For more information see Ball, *In the Days of Victorio;* Thrapp, *Victorio and the Mimbres Apaches;* and Chamberlain, *Victorio.* For history of the female side of the family, see Boyer and Gayton, *Apache Mothers and Daughters.*

6. A Bedonkohe Apache who became an inspiring leader of the Warm Springs Tribe. For more information, see Sweeney, *Mangas Coloradas.*

7. Stockel, personal conversation with Saenz, July 2008. Quoted in the *Western Historical Quarterly* 39, no. 4 (2008): 522–23.

8. Sister Juanita's interview is in *On the Bloody Road to Jesus,* 262–64.

9. One of the Mescalero Apache enterprises is cattle.

10. For more information, see Stockel, "Rocks, Waters, Earth: Chiricahua Apache Spiritual Geography," 18–27.

11. For more information, see Stockel, *Chiricahua Apache Women and Children: Safekeepers of the Heritage.*

Conversation: Kathleen Kanseah

1. Hopkins Smith Sr. was born a child prisoner of war at Fort Sill, Oklahoma, on February 21, 1901, the son of Oswald Smith and Gertrude Cleeneh Smith, also prisoners of war. The family was released from prisoner of war status in 1913. They moved to Whitetail, a site on the Mescalero Apache Reservation, with about two hundred newly freed other Chiricahua Apaches.

2. Carrizo is a site on the reservation.

3. Jasper Kanseah Sr. was Geronimo's nephew and approximately thirteen years old at the time of surrender in 1886.

4. Navajo country encompasses a vast area of the Four Corners—the site where New Mexico, Arizona, Colorado, and Utah meet.

5. The puberty ceremony, a most sacred event, is held annually to mark the passage of maidens into womanhood.

6. The puberty ceremony attracts many tribal members and visitors as well as vendors who offer a wide variety of fast foods, jewelry, and t-shirts.

7. The son of Chief Chihuahua who surrendered in April of 1886. As a child prisoner of war, Eugene was released in 1913 and moved to Whitetail on the Mescalero Apache Reservation where, with Asa Daklugie, he became a young leader of the newly freed Chiricahua Apaches. He is revered today.

8. Here Kathleen Kanseah is talking about the Mountain Spirit Dancers who are an essential part of the puberty ceremony and other sacred rituals.

9. A village that abuts the southern border of the reservation.

10. Trinity Site, where the bomb was tested, is part of the White Sands Missile Range, only about one hundred miles from the reservation.

11. A significant portion of the puberty ceremony is conducted inside "the big tipi," which is exactly what it is.

12. At the time of the interview, Carleton Naiche-Palmer, a direct descendant of Cochise, was president.

Conversation: Edward Little

1. Wendell Chino was a longtime president of the Mescalero Apache tribe.

2. The Ford Foundation's mission is to strengthen democratic values, reduce poverty and injustice, promote international cooperation, and advance human achievement. For more information, see http://www.fordfound.org.

3. As this is written, Carleton Naiche-Palmer has been president of the Mescalero Apache Tribe for one year.

4. Founded in 1944 in response to termination and assimilation policies forced on tribal governments, NCAI stresses the need for unity and cooperation among tribal governments for the protection of their treaty and sovereign rights. The NCAI also works to inform the public and Congress on the governmental rights of American Indians and Alaska Natives. For more information, see http://www.ncai.org.

5. The Bureau of Indian Affairs (BIA) is the oldest bureau of the U.S. Department of the Interior. Established in 1824, the BIA currently provides services directly or through contracts, grants, or compacts to approximately 1.7 million American Indians and Alaska Natives. For more information, see http://www.doi.gov/bureaus/bia.cfm.

6. The casino is part of the Inn of the Mountain Gods, a Mescalero Apache enterprise.

7. Truth or Consequences, New Mexico.

8. Sister Juanita Little, a Franciscan nun.

9. The Indian Community Action Program.

10. Joseph Little, an Albuquerque attorney.

11. New Mexico's senior senator, retired after three decades, in 2009.

12. As this is being written, the reference is to Bill Richardson, governor of New Mexico.

13. Ski Apache is a Mescalero Apache enterprise.

Conversation: Claudine Saenz

1. Chino was the longtime president of the Mescalero Apache Tribe.
2. Cleghorn became the chairperson of the Fort Sill Apache Tribe.
3. The Consolidated Omnibus Reconciliation Act of 1986.

Conversation: Sister Juanita

1. In November 2006 Sister Juanita wrote a letter to the president and Tribal Council requesting permission to contact students attending local schools as a first step in developing "a central tracking system that would identify drop outs and habitual truants and bring them to the attention of the appropriate authorities. [By] doing this we hope to reduce risk factors that prevent school age children from utilizing available educational opportunities." She never received an answer.

Conversation: Joey Padilla

1. An area on the reservation.
2. Raising cattle is an enterprise of the Mescalero Apache Tribe. Cow Camp is located high on one of the reservation's mountains and is the base from which the enterprise is run.
3. An area on the reservation.
4. The Waste Isolation Pilot Project near Carlsbad, New Mexico.
5. The median age on the reservation is eighteen years old.
6. For more information, see interview with Sister Juanita Little.
7. An Apache cultural/religious icon.

Conversation: Depree Shadowwalker

1. This reference is to "blood quantum," the total percentage of blood that is tribal native due to bloodline, determined by standards set by the government. Some Apaches believe it was created to exclude tribal members from receiving benefits. Morally sensitive people believe it is racist, as do I.
2. As this is being written, Ellen Bigrope is the curator at the Mescalero Apache Cultural Center, located on the reservation near the tribal offices.
3. The political slogan of the mid-1800s that conveyed the belief that "Americans are destined by divine providence to expand their national domain." (Lamar, *The New Encyclopedia of the American West,* 676).
4. Literally speaking, Shadowwalker may be correct when she notes "without the parents' permission." Still, many children from the Mescalero Apache Reservation went to boarding schools in Santa Fe and Albuquerque, both government and religious schools.

Conversation: Alfred LaPaz

1. Site of a famous gunfight between the Lincoln County Regulators and buffalo hunter Buckshot Roberts. Billy the Kid was one of the Regulators. For more information,

see http://en.wikipedia.org/wiki/Gunfight_of_Blazer's_Mills, and Blazer, *Santana: War Chief of the Mescalero Apache,* 41–55.

2. An acronym for Reduction in Force.

Conversation: Debi Martinez

1. New Mexico School for the Blind and Visually Handicapped, Alamogordo, New Mexico.

2. This reference is to Cochise's grandson.

3. Ussen is the Apache name for Creator.

4. Historical trauma has been defined as unresolved grief originating from the loss of lives, land, and vital aspects of native culture promulgated by the European conquest of the Americas. It is transmitted across the generations much like physical characteristics.

5. Joseph Geronimo and his brother Harlyn may or may not be direct descendants of the famous American hero. Controversy exists as to whether the bloodline is accurate.

Conversation: Elisa Yuzos

1. Dulce, New Mexico is home to the Jicarilla Apaches.

2. The only treaty between the United States and the Apache Indians that has been ratified and is in effect is dated July 1, 1852. It does not provide for medical purposes. A treaty dated June 14, 1855 promises U.S. payments for 1856–82, part of which might be used at the president's discretion for many purposes, including medical. That treaty was never ratified and is not in effect.

Conversation: Dan Kanseah Jr.

1. The Inn of the Mountain Gods is a 4 star destination resort and casino on the Mescalero Apache Reservation.

2. Recognizing the truancy problem, the Tribal Council adopted Tribal Ordinance 08–05 in August of 2008. The ordinance amends the Children's Code in order to provide measures to combat truancy and educational neglect, reinforce parental control, and protect school-age children residing on the Mescalero Apache Reservation and/or attending the Mescalero Apache School as well as school-age tribal members resident off the reservation, whether they attend the Mescalero School or another school. Enforcement began immediately and continues.

Conversation: Kiana Mangas

1. Ball, *Indeh: An Apache Odyssey.*

2. Two leaders on the Mescalero Apache Reservation who emerged after the prisoners of war were released in 1913.

3. A large range in southeastern Arizona.

4. One of the most famous Apache chiefs. For more information, see Sweeney, *Mangas Coloradas: Chief of the Chiricahua Apaches.*

5. The most famous chief of the Warm Springs Apaches. For more information, see Ball, *In the Days of Victorio;* Chamberlain, *Victorio;* and Thrapp, *Victorio and the Mimbres Apaches.*

6. Victorio's sister, a legendary woman warrior around whom a great many myths swirl.

Epilogue

1. The exception was Eve Ball's *Indeh: An Apache Odyssey,* published in 1980.

2. "Culture" defines and reflects the physical, emotional, and spiritual experiences of a people. A culture is dynamic, alive, and active, always changing through adaptation and adjustments. It is these activities that have created the twenty-first-century culture on the Mescalero Apache Reservation today.

3. For more information, see Stockel, *Salvation through Slavery,* and Stockel, *On the Bloody Road to Jesus.*

4. For more information, see Stockel, *Survival of the Spirit.*

5. Sonnichsen, *The Mescalero Apaches,* 114–18, 124.

6. Lipan Apache Tribe. At http://en.wikipedia.org/wiki/Lipan_Apache.

7. Stockel, *Shame and Endurance,* 153.

BIBLIOGRAPHY

Books

Ball, Eve. *In the Days of Victorio: Recollections of a Warm Springs Apache.* Tucson: University of Arizona Press, 1981.

———. *Indeh: An Apache Odyssey.* Provo, UT: Brigham Young University Press, 1980.

Blazer, Almer N. *Santana: War Chief of the Mescalero Apache.* Edited by A. R. Pruit. Taos, N.Mex.: Dog Soldier Press, 1999.

Bosque Redondo Memorial. *The Story of Bosque Redondo.* Fort Sumner, N.Mex.: Fort Sumner State Monument, n.d.

Boyer, Ruth McDonald, and Narcissus Duffy Gayton. *Apache Mothers and Daughters.* Norman: University of Oklahoma Press, 1992.

Chamberlain, Kathleen P. *Victorio: Apache Warrior and Chief.* Norman: University of Oklahoma Press, 2007.

Hoijer, Harry. *Chiricahua and Mescalero Apache Texts.* Chicago: University of Chicago Press, 1938.

Kidwell, Clara Sue, Homer Noley, and George "Tink" Tinker. *A Native American Theology.* Maryknoll, N.Y.: Orbis Books, 2001.

Lamar, Howard, ed. *The New Encyclopedia of the American West.* New Haven, Conn.: Yale University Press, 1998.

Opler, Morris. *An Apache Lifeway: The Economic, Social, and Religious Institutions of the Chiricahua Indians.* Chicago: University of Chicago Press, 1941.

Sonnichsen, C. L. *The Mescalero Apaches.* Norman: University of Oklahoma Press, 1958.

Stockel, H. Henrietta. *Chiricahua Apache Women and Children: Safekeepers of the Heritage.* College Station: Texas A&M University Press, 2000.

———. *On the Bloody Road to Jesus: Christianity and the Chiricahua Apaches.* Albuquerque: University of New Mexico Press, 2004.

———. *Salvation through Slavery: Chiricahua Apaches and Priests on the Spanish Colonial Frontier.* Albuquerque: University of New Mexico Press, 2008.

———. *Shame and Endurance: The Untold Story of the Chiricahua Apache Prisoners of War.* Tucson: University of Arizona Press, 2004.

———. *Survival of the Spirit: Chiricahua Apaches in Captivity.* Reno: University of Nevada Press, 1993.

———. *Women of the Apache Nation: Voices of Truth.* Reno: University of Nevada Press, 1991.

Sweeney, Edwin R. *Mangas Coloradas: Chief of the Chiricahua Apaches.* Norman: University of Oklahoma Press, 1998.

Thrapp, Dan L. *Victorio and the Mimbres Apaches.* Norman: University of Oklahoma Press, 1974.

Articles

Stockel, H. Henrietta. "Rocks, Waters, Earth: A Chiricahua Apache Spiritual Geography." *Journal of the West* 46, no. 4 (2007): 18–27.

Stolley, Richard B. "Postcard: Las Cruces: An Epic Journey to the Edge of Space." *Time* magazine, December 14, 2009, 10.

Interviews, Discussions, and Conversations

Kanseah, Dan, Jr. Interview with author, December 6, 2007.

Kanseah, Kathleen. Interview with Marian Kelley, January 12, 2008.

LaPaz, Alfred. Interview with author, June 11, 2008.

Little, Edward Michael. Interview with author, September 25, 2008.

Little, Sister Juanita, OFM. Interview with author, December 5, 2007.

Mangas, Kiana. Interview with author, January 30, 2009.

Martinez, Debi. Interview with author, September 18, 2008.

Padilla, Joey. Interview with author, April 14, 2008.

Saenz, Claudine. Telephone discussion with author, October 20, 2007.

———. Interview with author, December 4, 2007.

———. Personal conversation with author, July 2008.

Shadowwalker, Depree. Interview with author, February 25, 2008.

Shay, Larry. Interview with author, June 11, 2008.

Yuzos, Eliza. Interview with author, January 10, 2008.

Internet

Bureau of Indian Affairs. At http://www.doi.gov/bureaus/bia.cfm.

Ford Foundation. At http://www.fordfound.org.

Gunfight of Blazer's Mills. At http://en.wikipedia.org/wiki/Gunfight_of_Blazer's_Mills.

Lipan Apache Tribe. At http://en.wikipedia.org/wiki/Lipan_Apache.

National Congress of American Indians. At http://www.ncai.org.

Trinity Atomic Web Site. At http://www.cddc.vt.edu/host/atomic/trinity/trinity1.html.

INDEX

Volumes in the Elma Dill Russell Spencer Series in the West and Southwest:

1. *Aspects of the American West: Three Essays*, Joe B. Frantz
2. *The Trader on the American Frontier: Myth's Victim*, Howard R. Lamar
3. *America's Frontier Culture: Three Essays*, Ray A. Billington
4. *How Did Davy Die?* Dan E. Kilgore
5. *The Grave of John Wesley Hardin: Three Essays on Grassroots History*, C. L. Sonnichsen
6. *Juan Davis Bradburn: A Reappraisal of the Mexican Commander of Anahuac*, Margaret Swett Henson
7. *Civil War Recollections of James Lemuel Clark*, L. D. Clark, ed.
8. *The Texas Longhorn: Relic of the Past, Asset for the Future*, Donald E. Worcester
9. *Red Hole in Time*, Muriel Marshall
10. *Travels in Mexico and California*, A. B. Clarke
11. *The Mexican War Journal and Letters of Ralph W. Kirkham*, Robert. R. Miller
12. *Regional Studies: The Interplay of Land and People*, Glen E. Lich
13. *An Immigrant Soldier in the Mexican War*, Frederick Zeh
14. *Where Rivers Meet: Lore from the Colorado Frontier*, Muriel Marshall
15. *Massacre on the Lordsburg Road: A Tragedy of the Apache Wars*, Marc Simmons
16. *Geronimo's Kids: A Teacher's Lessons on the Apache Reservation*, Robert S. Ove and H. Henrietta Stockel
17. *Defiant Peacemaker: Nicholas Trist in the Mexican War*, Wallace Ohrt
18. *Life among the Texas Indians: The WPA Narratives*, David La Vere
19. *The Plains Indians*, Paul H. Carlson
20. *The Conquest of the Karankawas and the Tonkawas, 1821–1859: A Study in Social Change*, Kelly F. Himmel
21. *Chiricahua Apache Women and Children: Safekeepers of the Heritage*, H. Henrietta Stockel
22. *Hispanics in the Mormon Zion, 1912–1999*, Jorge Iber
23. *Comanche Society: Before the Reservation*, Gerald Betty
24. *True Women and Manifest Destiny*, Adrienne Caughfield
25. *The Robertson, the Sutherlands, and the Making of Texas*, Anne Sutherland
26. *Life Along the Border,* Maria Eugenia Cotera
27. *Lone Star Pasts: Memory and History in Texas,* Gregg Cantrell and Elizabeth Hayes Turner
28. *The Secret War for Texas*, Stuart Reid
29. *Colonial Natchitoches,* Burton and Smith
30. *Yeomen, Sharecroppers, and Socialists,* Kyle G. Wilkison
31. *More Zeal Than Discretion,* Jimmy L. Bryan
32. *On the Move,* S. R. Martin
33. *The Texas That Might Have Been,* Margaret Swett Henson, edited by
34. *Tejano Leadership in Mexican and Revolutionary Texas,* Jesús F. de la Teja
35. *The Texas Left,* Cullen and Wilkison
36. *How Did Davy Die? And Why Do We Care So Much?,* Kilgore and Crisp